RNterprise!

90 Day Success Plan for New Nurse Entrepreneurs

10 Steps to Start Up

By
Michelle Greene Rhodes, MHS, RN

This program was designed for the professional nurse or health care professional who aspires to take his or her knowledge outside of the setting of the traditional nurse. If you desire to fulfill a calling that only starting your own business can fulfill, then this book is for you!   Michelle

Chapters

Foreword by Albert Rhodes, Jr.

Having served in the US Air Force for 22 years, I've learned some important truths. I've learned that there's a right way and a wrong to do everything in the military, that leadership can be taught and how to act without fear of failure. In a way, entrepreneurship is not unlike the military, and my time in the Air Force has surely informed the way I do business.

I've been married to Michelle for five years now, and I've seen her transform her own career into a thriving entrepreneurship. I watch her every day, as we work from home together, as she helps to transform the lives of her clients. Part of what I think makes her successful is that she, too, believes there is a right and wrong way to tackle the challenges of starting a business. Her "right way" is based on a strong passion that clients realize their lives' purpose or souls' mission. The "right way" to approach your job is as if it's not simply a job, but what inspires you and makes you feel alive.

Michelle coaches her clients to do just this. She infuses them with a confidence that they don't have when they start working with her. At the outset, many think that they are trapped in their circumstances; they believe their options, as a nurse, are limited to hospitals and similar facilities, and that their only choice is WHICH facility. But I've watched Michelle take them from that thought to a belief in their unlimited potential. It's amazing to see, and seems like the "right way" to approach life.

When I was in the military, I learned that leadership could be taught, but not everyone is aware that it's not an innate trait. Michelle, too, has the uncanny ability to teach leadership. As a mentor and coach, her energy and dedication is effervescent and contagious, and through this natural style, she literally gives her clients the tools to be leaders, while supporting them every step of the way.

I became a father for the first time when I adopted Michelle's son (and now our son), Jon. I became a biological father for the first time at age 46, when Michelle and I had our daughter, Ali. I can tell you there is no situation where you feel the fear of failure more than when become a parent. You worry constantly and wonder non-stop about whether the decisions you're making for your children are right or wrong. Both Michelle and I know that it's healthy to worry and to feel fear, but that fear of failure is no reason to NOT do something. We persevere in spite of that fear. And that makes us better. That's what we do in our family, and that's what we do in our businesses. And that's what Michelle inspires her clients to do - to persevere even when they think they might fail. Because...what if they don't? What if they rise to the challenge?

I absolutely love being an entrepreneur in my staffing agency and my travel business. There is nothing better than getting to work beside my wife every day, doing what I love and being available for my children when they need me.

I also could not give up this new-found freedom. We love traveling, watching sunsets and walking on the beach. I wouldn't trade it for the world, and I believe that everyone should have that opportunity if they feel the call.

But I also know that it's difficult to do so in a vacuum. While in the military, I had top notch mentors, and at the same time, Michelle had excellent mentors on her journey as well. Now she is that person for others, and it's so inspiring. If you have any desire at all to go out on your own and stop pouring your heart and soul working for someone else, when you could be pouring it into your own business, but are scared or worried or just not sure where to start, then not only is this book for you, Michelle is for you.

I personally invite you to step into this journey. Peruse this book. Talk to Michelle. Attend her events. Live your life the "right way." Live it for you. Live your life's purpose today. You're at a great starting point right now. Just turn the page.

The Hubby,

Al

Introduction

Chapter 1 – About this Book

If you're reading this book, I'm assuming that you are a nurse or health care practitioner who loves what you do and who has always found great satisfaction in the role you've had in helping people. In addition, I'm sure that you're probably very proud of your credentials and your experience, and you should be. You have a valuable background that is a huge asset to society. But if you're here, I'm also assuming that, despite your general job satisfaction, you've found there is still something missing. This exact missing piece could be a bit different for everyone and we'll address this and how to obtain the missing piece later, but if you're itching to move elsewhere, or craft a fresh start somehow, it's because somewhere there is a part of you that is not satisfied in your career.

The nursing industry is a stressful place. Most of us set out on this career trajectory because we feel an inherent desire to help others and to provide care and comfort to those in need. Of course, we also enjoy the practical aspects of the field, but most likely the driving force behind why you became a nurse lies in the difference you make in the lives of your patients. You may even feel that helping others is your calling or life's purpose.

Nursing is an industry unlike any other. We help others constantly, but often our own bodies suffer because of it. There are a few obstacles in particular that arise in the conventional nurse's role:

- Long Shifts – Most nurses spend many hours on the job, and these hours are not spent sitting down, working on a computer. Nurses spend hours on their feet, tending to others.

Many nurses opt for working three 12-hour days instead of more days with fewer hours. And because hospitals never close, nurses are usually required to work holidays and nights. Anything is manageable for a short, fixed amount of time, and often this schedule sounds appealing to us, especially when we're young and just starting out; but long-term, this takes a toll on our bodies and minds.

- Others Come First – The entire premise of nursing is that we're caring for others' needs above our own. It is literally our job to put our needs aside for those for which we are caring. This is both very rewarding and very draining. After all, if we don't take care of ourselves, we will eventually have nothing left to give to others.

- Short-Staffed Hospitals and Facilities – Because nurses are in such high demand, there is always a need for our work, but often, not enough nurses to cover all shifts. This forces hospitals to work its nurses to the max. It seems as though there are always more patients than nurses, and so we are pressured into helping both because management insists AND because we do generally want to help when we can. More often than not, we will sacrifice our own needs for the good of the hospital and the patients. Not to mention patient survey results that seem to force decision making.

- Emotionally Taxing – Caring for sick and dying patients is an incredibly emotionally taxing career. Constantly, nurses are exposed to heartbreaking situations and required to call upon their mental and emotional stamina to deal with terminal patients and tragic accidents. It's not a career for the faint of heart, but even the most resilient of nurses can find himself/herself emotionally weak after dealing with so much sadness.

So, how can nurses navigate these obstacles and find satisfaction in their work, while still continuing to persist in the field that they love?

First, it's important to look inside yourself to determine where the weakness lies. Are you feeling like a hostage to your schedule, with not enough time to sufficiently recuperate and be ready to give of yourself again? Do you feel stressed because you're doing too much? Do you feel disengaged and burnt out, as if you have nothing left to give? Maybe you simply wish your job had more flexibility. And, if nurses are so needed and so valuable, then why does it seem like you're always at someone else's mercy? If that's the case, shouldn't there be a way for you to be more selective about how you spend the hours of your life?

It's also important to remember that you are so much more than a nurse. On this journey, it's important for you to recognize all of the other things you are in addition to being a nurse. Are you a mother, a father, a friend, a coach, a sister, a brother, a daughter, a wife, a husband? You get the picture. Your patients are very important to you, of course, but your life can only be well balanced if all the relationships that are important to you are in a healthy state as well. In addition, you must also feel spiritually fulfilled. Do you currently have time to attend mass and to satisfy all of your spiritual commitments? Or are you drained from your week and finding even what normally fills you up and provides inspiration to be drawing on your reserves?

The goal of this book is to assist you on your journey of creating a nursing career that is founded on your terms. Nursing is your calling and your life's purpose, but you want to satisfy this calling and simultaneously create an RNterprise that is fulfilling and practical. I will take you, step by step, through the process of turning your passion for helping others into an entrepreneurial endeavor that will, ultimately, be satisfying to you - on all levels. As we move through this book, we will look at the whole picture of you. We will discover what is most important for you to have in your life, and we will create a practical way for you to achieve that. I'll take you through the steps and logistics of setting up a business, and will answer questions, based on my own experience, in the process. We'll cover everything from branding your business to networking to social media.

This book is formatted as a chronological journey to entrepreneurship. I've set the chapters up in a way that, if followed in order, can have you working as a self-sufficient entrepreneur by the end. You can't very well get clients without first having a brand and a budget. Well...you can, but your success and professionalism will be compromised. That's why I've tried to lay out this book in an order where each chapter builds on the next. We want to create something strong, organized and productive by the time we are done.

The most important take-away from this book is that you can do what you love without having to make unreasonable sacrifices. You can create a career for yourself that has purpose, flexibility and balance. Nurses have incredible value in our society. Our skills are needed, but, somehow, also often taken advantage of. I will teach you how to use this value to empower yourself and to leverage your skills and talent, rather than submitting to the expectations and impositions common in the healthcare industry.

Now, let's get started.

Chapter 2

The Vision & The Details – Days 1-5

Figuring out where to start can be very daunting. After all, there are so many steps to starting your own business; how do you decide where to begin? What's most important to have in order first? Are there specific items that you absolutely need to have in place before you take your first client? And, equally harrowing, when does too much planning start to become your enemy? When do you stop planning and start doing, or risk being forever preparing?

Envision it

Now that you have the itch for self-employment, it's important to sit down and sketch out what you want your overall life to look like. This initial step means envisioning the big picture. I call this "see it before you see it," aka 'faith'.

So, we're going to ignore the smaller details to start. First, I just want you to think a little wider in scope. Think about what is important for you to get out of this endeavor. Do you want more time to spend with your family, or focus on your relationship? Do you have a full-time job that you would need to leave immediately, or could you make less dramatic changes and ease into full-time self-employment? Do you need to consider finances and how you will support yourself during the transition? Is there a certain element of your current job that you either love or hate and how do you want to incorporate or eliminate that in the position you create for yourself? This is all an activity to help you find your WHY.

There are a few specific categories at which you should take a look in order to help determine your long-term priorities. Once there is a clear sense of what's most important in your vision of the future, it will be clear what steps need to be taken in order to make it a reality. Basically, we're looking to create a healthy work/life balance. No matter what your career, if you're spending more time working than spending with your family, you'll never be happy. The key is to find out what that work/life balance is so that we can set out to achieve it.

Your Health

How is your current health? Are your current long hours and responsibilities impacting your well-being? Here are some of the major elements to consider.

Sleep

One of the hallmarks of a typical nursing position is long hours. Because none of us exists only to work, we have other responsibilities to take care of when we get home from long shifts. This could mean that the area where we cut corners is sleep. One night with little sleep is manageable for anyone, but when it gets to the point that you're chronically shortening your sleep (six hours or less on regular basis), you're starting to compromise your own health.

As a fellow nurse, I'm sure that you know the effects of sleep deprivation, but I'll list them here because, as we become sleep-deprived, it's easy to say that we've adapted to simply living on little sleep; however, this simply isn't true. We can trick ourselves into believing that we're getting more done, but studies show that as impervious as we believe ourselves to be to insufficient sleep, our performance and mental alertness are, indeed, impaired.

Sleep deprivation results in:

- Slower reaction times

- Increased likelihood of accidents and injuries

- Compromised immune system

- Higher risk for heart-related diseases, high blood pressure, stroke and diabetes

- Decreased libido

- Higher susceptibility to depression and anxiety

- Decreased memory

- Weight gain

Pain

Nursing requires long hours on our feet, heavy lifting and lots of physically exhausting work. Patient handling is a dangerous endeavor. Nurses can suffer strains, sprains and other injuries by overexertion, engaging in repetitive motions or anything as a result of an unexpected patient movement. Sometimes, with our hectic schedules and the pressure to ensure every patient is taken care of, we open ourselves up to getting injured on the job because we are in a hurry.

Sometimes, it doesn't matter what precautions we take - the nature of a physically taxing job is the risk of injury. Chronic back pain and wrist or other joint pain can be common in our profession.

Do you have chronic pain that is a result of long hours and jam-packed schedule? What would your business look like in order for you to avoid the practices that are causing your pain and discomfort?

Stress

In addition to the physical demands of nursing, the nature of the career is emotionally demanding on a consistent basis. Nursing is an occupation, which requires numerous interactions with patients each day, many of whom are emotionally strenuous to deal with. There is a chronic stress associated with all of these interactions that, if not dealt with in some way, can result in nurse burnout. Burnout is characterized by emotional exhaustion, depersonalization and reduced personal accomplishment.[1]

Granted, it's not just working with the patient that's stressful for nurses. There are also schedules, staffing, decision-making,

---

[1] C. Maslach, *Burnout-The Cost of Caring* (Englewood Cliffs, New Jersey: Prentice-Hall, 1982), p. 3.

technology and the ever present human suffering that can tax our emotional reserves.

If you're feeling stressed in your current position, it's important to identify the source of your stress. If your stress is mostly a result of ridiculous schedules, being understaffed or unreasonable expectations, we can definitely eliminate these by moving into entrepreneurship. If you're stressed because the level of human suffering is taking its toll on you, we still can create a successful entrepreneurship, but it might be prudent to fashion a career that would minimize your interaction with these difficult situations.

We'll touch on this more later, but not every nurse entrepreneurship means working with patients; or at least, working with terminal patients. There are plenty of nursing career ideas where you can utilize your knowledge and experience without incorporating stressors. For example, you could specialize in childbirth, maternity or lactation in order to keep a more uplifting note to your work, or you could adopt a more retail-like function, selling affordable scrubs or medical equipment. You could specialize in areas that involve health insurance paperwork, medical supplies or legal consult.

The important thing for you to do right now, however, is to determine where you are in terms of on the job stress, and then decide where you want to be on that scale in the future. All of this bigger picture knowledge is going to help you make more specific decisions later.

Your Relationship

Whether or not you currently have a relationship is not important. If you DO have a relationship, are you dedicating the amount of time and energy that you want? And if you DON'T have a relationship, do you want to have one? Do you have the time to pursue one, or is your life so full of work that you don't have the time...even if you wanted to?

Immersing yourself in work is a great distraction from the fact that you may not be happy with your current relationship or lack of relationship. Oftentimes, as long as we have the excuse that we're working, it seems that we can rationalize whatever state our love life is in. Society seems to tell us that work is more important than relationships. After all - relationships count as fun, don't they? And fun should be a luxury, once we're finished with our day's work.

This outlook is more of an illusion than a reality. First of all, relationships are not necessarily going to be any fun if you don't put in the time. If what we're calling "fun" or meaningful personal interactions always come second, we lose what is actually the thing that provides us fuel to get through the work.

My point here is that in order to have a truly successful career - one that makes you happy - you must also have balance in your personal life, whatever that means to you. This might mean having a healthy relationship, dedicating yourself to spending a fair amount of time to finding this relationship, or it might mean focusing on yourself and your own interests so that, eventually, you are ready to enter into a relationship. Maybe you are a single parent, and none of that seems reasonable to fit into your schedule. If that's the case, let me ask you, for a moment, to suspend the needs of your children and think about your true long-term goals. We're just envisioning, after all. In an ideal world, what would you have the time for? Where do you see yourself in 3 years? In 5 years? In 10 years?

Before we create this nursing business, we have to have as accurate a picture as we can about what will make it the most satisfying for you. So, be truthful in what you envision. If you simply think that you don't have time to worry about a relationship right now - that you have to focus on your kids and starting a very flexible business - then that's what you will get. But you are the one creating this business and hold the keys to your future, so why not decide what you would want in an ideal world and start working towards it! That's the only way the ideal will become real. Remember that if you're happy in what you do, that reserve of joy and passion will trickle over into your personal life. Doing what you "think" is better for your children is not necessarily the answer. Doing what makes you happy, and is your passion, will undoubtedly show and extend out to all areas of your life. So, don't limit yourself because of your children; instead, show them how to live your life's purpose, so that all areas of your life are balanced and healthy.

Time

Time, or lack thereof, actually, is nearly everyone's biggest complaint. There is never enough time to do whatever it is we want. We should all try being a nurse, and then we'll really understand what it's like not to have any time for yourself.

It's important to take time now, at the outset of your endeavor, to decide what kind of "down time" will be ideal as you move forward. Do you want a lot of free time? Think about what you've already decided in regard to your health and relationship. Will you need a great deal of spare time to achieve these goals? Or are you actually the kind of person who doesn't do well with a lot of spare time? Some people do actually prefer to be busy and have jam-packed schedules as it fills them with a sense of purpose. If that's you, decide what you'd be doing in your ideal "busyness." In other words, do you love to volunteer, go the movies or theater; do you wish you had time to take dance classes?

Whatever it is, decide. You want time for _____ (fill in the blank). We will build your business so that you have time for that thing. Maybe that thing is sleep or traveling or Netflix. There's nothing wrong with doing nothing as long as it is what you choose. To choose nothing and sit around staring at your television is disheartening and unsatisfying, but if your goal is to have time to decompress watching your favorite show, then we can meet that goal and not feel guilty about it.

Business Management

Once your business is up and running, it will end up consisting of a lot of what you love and a lot of paperwork and admin. How do you envision yourself balancing these two elements? What do you want your typical workweek to look like? Will you take clients some days and work from home (doing marketing, paperwork and other business maintenance) other days? Might you want to grow to a point where you can hire someone to take care of that element for you? Do you want to work part-time or full-time and will that choice provide the required funds needed to do so? Are you the primary earner in your household or do you just need to make enough to supplement?

These are all important things to consider when you're outlining your business plan. Depending on what you require financially will determine whether you need only a couple of regular clients or if you need to find a way to appeal to a larger audience.

As I mentioned earlier, there are many routes that your business can take; it all depends on your specific interests, needs and desires. Maybe you only really love one aspect of your current generalist nursing role. What if you took that one thing and made it the essence of your business?

Oftentimes, Nurse Entrepreneurs make the mistake of thinking that they must generalize and offer everything to anyone in order to have the largest opportunity for earning potential. After all, you wouldn't want to limit your services, because then someone might not call you.

Wrong! Niches and specialties are a powerful thing. First off, you are only one person. Stretching yourself to meet the needs of every possible client is exactly how you got to the position that you're currently in. But even more so, there is a power that comes with specializing in a certain area. You become the expert in your chosen niche. For example, you want to specialize as a midwife/doula. You can focus all your energy, funds and time on marketing to the audience most likely to get pregnant – young, adult women. You've just narrowed your market considerably. So instead of being a good choice out of a list of hundreds of other nurse generalists, you become the best choice only for those who need a doula. Think of the power of the referrals you'll have. If one young woman requires a doula, her friends are likely around a similar age and stage of life, so you'll be the name she shares with her friends when they become pregnant. That's just an example, but this premise translates to any niche.

If you were just a general nurse with no specialty, where would you even start marketing? You'd have to spread your resources much thinner to make a similar impact in the pool of potential clients.

The possibilities are only as limited as your imagination. If you love to travel, you can leverage your desire to travel to your clients and focus on housebound patients. Maybe you can find other nurses and form a group that provides in home care. With a group, you can create your own schedules, and always have someone available. What a great service that would be! Or, if you love paperwork and have developed a keen sense for the industry, you can create a business dedicated to helping clients navigate the insurance industry. Maybe you want to focus on children or seniors, or maybe you focus on finding those with aging parents who need help with the next step. Perhaps your focus is on nutrition or health coaching. Or maybe you want to start a monogrammed scrub line that is custom, unique and affordable. All you need to do is hone in on what you love most about nursing, assess whether there is a need for this offering and then build it.

Again, we're still in the idea and brainstorming stage, so don't get bogged down by thinking about the details just yet. First, it's important to let your mind wander and to get excited about the opportunities. We'll discuss the logistics of taxes, funds and naming your business in a bit, but first I want you to allow yourself to get a bit wild and to think big. Your ultimate goal has to be something that you love and has to inspire you. It's going to be your vision that will continue to provide inspiration when things get hard, or setbacks arise, so it's important that the end goal fulfills you on all levels. That's how you're going to maintain your dedication and motivation when things get hard. Because they will. That's the nature of business. Just because you'll be working for yourself doesn't mean that each day will be filled with bliss. The difference will be that you'll know that you're working toward something that is fulfilling and satisfying to you, and that its realization will satisfy on all levels.

Thinking & Focusing

One setback that most of us encounter on the road to self-employment is how to stay focused. It's incredibly easy to get swept up in the day-to-day tasks that steal our time. How can you be sure that you'll be good at being your own boss? Will you get distracted, lose focus and end up wasting funds? Will you be closing your doors right after you open them?

These are all reasonable fears, but nothing to dwell on. And, in fact, the reason that you will be a good boss for yourself is because whatever you do, or don't do, directly affects you. If you're a bad boss, you'll let yourself sleep in every day, you won't get anything done and you won't have clients or money as a result. So, you won't do it for long once you see that it's affecting your bottom line.

Picture yourself working as a pastry chef in a fancy restaurant. If you don't show up, or if you do a mediocre job, no one is really going to know that it's your fault that the chocolate cake is a little dry that night. But if you're having people to your house, and you're putting a dessert in front of your guests, you're naturally going to make sure that it comes out amazing because everyone is going to know that, whatever the cake tastes like - good or bad - it's all you. So, you can bet that you're going to make sure it comes out great.

The same is true for your nursing business. You will have an intrinsic desire to work hard to achieve your ends...because they are YOUR ends. At the same time, don't make the mistake of focusing too intensely on every little thing. Focusing too much on the details, or getting things just right, can foil your business as well. Sometimes, in fact, it is easier for us to continue working on the website, or the plan, just so we can avoid actually doing it. We get off the hook by telling ourselves that we spent all day working on our business without actually moving out of our comfort zone into scoring the actual clients and doing the actual work.

Keeping your goal in mind and reaffirming your life's purpose every morning will help you adhere to your path. Putting the time and effort into this worthwhile endeavor is something you owe to yourself; by doing the work, you'll be giving yourself a better life.

Do It

Now that you've taken some time to envision what you want your whole life to look like once your business is up and functioning, it's time to move into the actual, physical steps you need to take to get there. For some, the actual envisioning of an alternate lifestyle is the daunting part. For others, the daunting part is actually finding the first step. I'm here to take the uncertainty out of the process. Let's take a look at what to do now that we know where we want to go.

Name Selection

The name of your business is an important decision.

Some things to consider when deciding on a name:

- **Make it pronounceable and easy to remember** – Consider that much of your business will be referral based. Your clients can't refer to what they can't pronounce or remember. It needs to be something that sticks with them. If you have a catchy name, that's great. Make use of it. If you have a first or last name that's difficult to spell or say, consider other alternatives first. Remember - your website will also likely be a version of your business name, so a challenging name could translate to lost business when prospective customers are required to spell it out. Also consider if your first and last name are extremely common, causing a Google search to return handfuls of others with the same name. In this case, your business name is going to be the differentiating factor.

- **Think of your product or service and location** – Make sure you think about your target market. What are they typing into search engines when they are looking for your product or service? Can you capitalize on some of those terms? Remember - you want to stand out, but you still want to have a name that makes sense in your industry. Does the name you're considering accurately describe your company? Will using your location (town or street) hamper you down the road if you should choose to relocate or grow?

- **Don't be too cute** – A clever name sometimes works because it becomes memorable, but steer clear of being too cute. Remember - you need to appear reputable and professional.

Cute names work well when the product or service offered is also a cute. It could be helpful to decide on three adjectives that describe you and your business. You can also sketch out a mission statement or description of your services. Write this down, and then brainstorm names that evoke what you just wrote. If you're going to focus on some modern treatment, you might want a name that sounds a little futuristic and modern, but if you're going to focus on being a doula or providing mobile care, you might want to evoke the 19th century feeling of the house call. Essentially, decide what you want your name to say about you; then make sure it does.

- **Be meaningful** – Is there any way to craft your business name to have added significance? For example, is your last name, town or street name also descriptive of an element of your business? If your last name is Swift and you also plan on providing care that is efficient and fast, Swift Nursing works in two ways to describe you.

- **Make sure it is not taken** – The last thing you want to do is come up with a name that can be easily confused with your competition. You want to stand out, not blend in. You can take a look at your competition to see what they're going by, but then make sure you come up with something fresh and different. Avoid the temptation to come up with something similar to your competition in order to benefit from their existing traffic. The intention here is inauthentic; forcing yourself into branding based on what someone else is doing will not ultimately aid in creating a cohesive, genuine brand for your company.

Once you decide upon your name, make sure that the domain is available. If it is taken, that doesn't mean you have to start from square one. See what business has your domain. If it's something totally unrelated to your business and is far away in location, it may be okay. For example, if you're looking to place an organic food order for a restaurant, you may try to type in, "United.com" to get to United Natural Foods, but you'd end up at the airline. That didn't stop United Natural Foods from sticking with that name, but they did have to come up with a different domain, so they use initials for their website. So, it's not necessarily a dealbreaker if your domain is taken, but if the person with your domain is another nurse who lives across town, then it might be wise to change. You'll just have to see who has your domain, and decide whether it makes more sense to change your domain or your business name.

Legal Entities

The first legal matter upon which you should decide when starting a business is how you will structure your business from a tax standpoint. You can read extensively about the differences among all of these structures at irs.gov and sba.gov, but I'll give you some general guidelines to help you determine how to make this decision.

Your options for structuring are sole proprietorship, partnership, C corporation, S corporation or LLC.

Take your time deciding which is the best option for you, and consider seeking professional advice from an attorney. Here is some general information on each.

Sole Proprietorship – Under a sole proprietorship, you retain all responsibility for the debts and obligations of the business. This will be the least costly structure, but will also offer the least protection. You and the business are essentially the same entity, so all profits and losses of the business are passed directly on to you as the individual. If you have assets, they could be affected if the business is sued or held liable for anything.

Partnership – A partnership is similar to a sole proprietorship but involves more than one person, so if you plan on starting your business with someone else, this is something to consider.

Neither a sole proprietorship, nor a partnership, requires you to file any paperwork to get started. Though these options are cheaper at the outset, financial consequences could have more gravity and more personal weight down the line. If anything should happen to the company, your personal assets, such as your house and car, could be at risk. However, if liability is not much of a concern for you and your business, this could be a good option.

Corporation – The main difference between the previous two options and a corporation is that when you make your business a corporation, it becomes an entity separate from you. Therefore your personal assets are no longer at risk if the business should be liable for something, as corporations receive limited liability protection against business losses and obligations. To become either a C corporation or an S corporation, you must file Articles of Incorporation with your state. The cost of doing this varies from state to state. Once you file these, you can register your business in that state.

Also, as far as taxes go, Sole Proprietorships and Partnerships are considered pass-through entities, meaning that the profits and losses get passed through directly to the individuals' income tax reports. Corporations, on the other hand, are double taxed. So, although there are more tax allowances for corporations, they require more paperwork and means you'll be double taxed.

Limited Liability Companies - This option blends together some of the features of the previous options. An LLC offers protection against liability, so that an individual's assets can't be touched in response to business dealings, but it is still considered a pass-through entity, and profits and losses move through to the individual's income tax report. Creating an LLC is more costly at the outset than a Sole Proprietorship or Partnership.

It's also important to consider how you'll be getting funding for your business as you consider which structure to go with. It is more difficult to find outside funding as a Sole Proprietor or Partnership than it is as a corporation or LLC. The main reason for this is because a Sole Proprietor or Partnership lacks a certain level of credibility, since there is no initial investment in incorporating or forming an LLC. This will make it more difficult to get business loans and could mean that you have to rely on personal savings to get started.

With this general information in mind, you can start to get a sense of what business structure makes the most sense for you and your business.

I highly recommend that you still consult with an accountant or attorney who can give you more in depth and personalized information. It's important to take the time at the outset to get this right so that you're not paying for your haste down the road. The specifics of what kind of nursing business you're starting, what your personal assets include, whether you're single or married and other personal information will determine which option makes the most sense for you. Please consult with your Attorney to determine what works best officially for your business.

Taxes

Once you decide on your business structure, it's time to register your business. If you are creating a corporation, you will need to file your Article of Incorporation. Otherwise, you will need to register your business name as a "Doing Business As." The rules for this vary a little from state to state. You can find more information by visiting the Small Business Administration website at sba.gov.

Once you register, determine if you need to obtain an Employer Identification Number; check the IRS website to find out if you need to do this. Registering online is free. Having a EIN will allow you to separate your personal and business finances and is essential if you plan on hiring others to work for you.

You can determine what tax responsibilities you have in your particular state at the sba.gov website. Also, at this point, you'll want to determine what kinds of licenses and permits are required in your state. You can find a checklist for this on the sba.gov website, as well. Please consult your CPA before, during and after start-upa of your business.

Office

Whatever your business looks like, if you're seeing patients in their homes and going out on the road, you will still need to set up an office or a consistent place where you can take care of the admin end of the business. If possible, I'd recommend avoiding taking your laptop to your couch and doing all your admin work in front of the television. Having an office will help you view this as a real and legit business, in addition to providing you with more organization. You'll want a place to keep your notes, files and calendar. Also, if you plan on writing off a portion of your rent on your taxes, you will need a designated area dedicated to your business. This could be a desk in the corner of the room, but not the coffee table.

It is tempting and feasible to use your cell phone as your business phone. I think a landline is something to consider on a case-by-case basis. If it makes sense to separate business from cell, than go ahead and do so. If you'll be on the road more often, and it makes more sense to use your cell for business, that's a good alternative. Just be mindful of your voicemail messages and keeping it professional. There are also services available that allow you to have a toll-free number that is routed to your cell phone. This way, on business cards and websites, you're not broadcasting your personal number, but still are able take the call conveniently on your cell.

You'll also want to consider whether you will need a fax machine and, therefore, a line dedicated to your fax. If scanning documents will work for you, you can consider getting a printer/scanner instead, which works by sending documents through email. There are also cheaper app options available that could replace spending initial funds on a scanner. You could hold off on deciding until you see what your needs will be. If you do need to scan or fax, any UPS, Fedex or Kinko's will allow you to do this for a fee. And local libraries might have free or cheaper options to send documents, so if you are unsure of what your needs will be, you can try these options and reassess in a few months if it's becoming too expensive or inconvenient.

Credit Card Transactions

Your business will greatly increase if you have the ability to process credit cards. There are two incredibly easy and affordable options available to you.

Set up a Square Account

A Square is a device that you can easily attach into the audio jack of your iPhone, Android, iPad, or tablet. The device then allows you to swipe a client's credit card. Transactions are subject to a small processing fee, and the transactions are processed through the Square's internal accounting system, then sent over to your attached bank account within a day.

Paypal

If you don't need to physically swipe a card, you can use Paypal to accept credit cards, whether or not the client has a Paypal account. You can either use Paypal's Virtual Terminal service to manually enter in credit cards, or you can link your Paypal to your business checking account.

Funding

Before you officially hang your shingle, it's important to decide how you will fund your business. Where you plan on getting your funding should be laid out in your business plan. The worst situation you could run into is to have spent a considerable amount of money starting up and then running out with few or no alternatives. Now you've poured money into an endeavor that can be putting you and your assets at risk.

The more prudent option is to have a clear sense of what capital you already have, in terms of personal savings and expendable income, and then determine how much you'll need until you can expect to see a profit from the business. If you have a significant other with a comfortable income and can afford to operate at a loss or breaking even for awhile, that's important to know at the outset. If you do not have this luxury, then you will need to outline other potential income sources in order to make ends meet.

The first step is to determine your monthly budget. What is your rent or mortgage? What are you monthly expenses? What can be trimmed and what can't? Are there specific, expected expenses coming up? Can you downsize in some ways to make room for fluctuations in your income?

Once you determine your cost of living, you can begin to look at what additional money you will need to earn so that you don't run out of capital. Perhaps you need to continue working part-time in order to make this business work. If that's the case, make a timeline with specific goals so that you can set dates for when you are able to phase out your part-time job. To go in without set dates could mean setting yourself up to get caught in the job. It's very easy to get stuck in a rut, but if you have real timelines in place, you can make sure that you're consistently taking the appropriate steps to get you where you need to go.

Let's take a look at a variety of possible funding options so that you know what your choices are. Some may be right for you, and some may not. It's important to remember that, sometimes, seeking funding can turn into a full time job in itself. You don't want to take on too much and risk neglecting the business, and your passion, because all of your time is required to raise funds.

Personal Savings

A hefty savings account is one means for financing a business. This is a great resource if you do, indeed, have a considerable savings account. Remember that you'll need to consider your entire situation. If your income is the only one in the household, your savings needs to be considerable enough to cover living expenses for at least six months, in addition to the amount of capital that you deemed necessary at the outset of your business. If your savings are smaller, consider a more aggressive savings plan for the next year or so as you plan to leave your current job or plan on supplementing personal savings with some other funding method.

Credit Cards

Credit Cards can be a great way to increase your spending power, but they can also be dangerous if not used properly. First of all, consider what your current credit score is and how much of your credit is already used. The better your credit score, the better chance you have at finding a low APR credit card. If your credit score is lower, you might end up accruing high interest rates and finance charges that you'll have to pay your way out of later. Do you trust your business to be generating enough profits to pay off your credit bills as they come in? If you spend beyond what you can handle, and fall behind on the payments, your credit score will take a beating. This can become a big deal when you need additional spending power down the road.

If you won't be able to pay much more than the minimum payment, you really can't afford to use a credit card. If you can pay most of the balance off by the end of the month, and mostly plan on using credit to open up cash flow, credit cards will be a safer bet.

Personal Loans

Getting a personal loan can be a great alternative to using an advance on your credit card or even simply using your credit card for all expenses. Generally, the interest rate on a personal loan will be considerably less than what it would be on a credit card, especially if you have decent credit. Shop around for the best rate. You don't have to accept the first offer you get. Once you're approved, you'll receive the approved amount and will then have an allotted amount of time to pay it back.

Business Loans

A second option in terms of loans is to apply for a business loan. There is a higher possibility for a larger allocation with a business loan as opposed to a personal loan. Business lenders, however, have more stipulations that must be met in order to approve the loan. Whereas a personal loan would simply be based on your credit score, a business loan will require information, including a business plan and business earnings. It may also be secured, meaning that it is attached to collateral.

You may be missing out on the chance to build credit for your business by taking out a personal loan to finance a business. This might be fine for your purposes at the outset, but down the road, as your business expands, a business loan will help build credit toward larger financing options.

When considering taking out either type of loan, it's best to consult a financial advisor to make sure that you're making the smartest decision for your purposes.

Venture Capitalist

I'd recommend seeking out a venture capitalist to invest in your business if you think that your particular idea is scalable and has large earning potential. A thing to remember is that venture capitalists have little interest in taking a brilliant idea and turning it into a business. Their main interest is taking viable businesses and turning them into billion dollar ventures. So, if there is potential for a large investment to transform your existing business into a multimillion-dollar generator, then seeking out a venture capitalist could be the way to go.

If your nursing entrepreneurship concept focuses more on you and the services you provide to a specific population, it might not be feasible as a million-dollar venture, because "your" services mean "your" time and that time is limited; but if your idea is more scalable, and is a more innovative concept, like perhaps an app where you can request a nurse at any time of day or a program that is franchise-able, that might be something that appeals to a venture capitalist. In that case, you'll want to have some market history to show to a venture capitalist as proof that there is interest and potential for growth.

Angel Investors

Angel Investors are similar to venture capitalists but rather than working for companies and investing business money, they are usually wealthy individuals who are investing in compelling business ideas that are important to them usually for a stake or equity in the business. An angel investor will be more likely to invest in the early stages of a business, whereas a venture capitalist wants to see proof of potential. Because they are individuals, however, they will usually have the ability to offer less, though still considerable, sums.

Grants

Grants are another option to secure funds to grow your business. The obvious benefit of a grant is that it is essentially free money that you don't have to pay back. There is, however, a possibility that you will have to report what you've used it for, and the grant process can be a long one. There are many stipulations when applying for grants, so you'll need to make sure you're thoroughly prepared for the process. The first step would be to find out what grants you qualify for, and then to go about gathering the necessary information and drafting your request.

Crowdfunding

With the explosion of the internet and social media, there is a relatively new option for generating funding for new business ideas - crowdfunding. Two popular sites are kickstarter and indiegogo. Crowdfunding could be a viable option for you, especially if your idea has some socially conscious element to it or is something that people would want to get behind and support. People love being part of something that is bigger than themselves, so if you can paint a picture of your business as something that could make a difference if it could reach a specific goal, then crowdfunding could be the way to go.

As you can see, there are plenty of ways to acquire capital for your business. If the nature of your business idea requires a large sum of initial capital to get going, I'd recommend trying one of these methods. In addition, I also recommend committing full-heartedly to your idea. A lot of power and the potential for doors opening come from simply believing in yourself and getting serious about your endeavor. By seeing your business as legitimate, worthwhile and valuable, you are indeed setting in motion for that to become so. If, on the other hand, you're evasive and wishy-washy about your intentions, and have one foot in and one foot out, that's exactly what you will get. Commit to your business, to your mission and to entrepreneurship. See yourself in the role and trust that you have something essential that your potential customers need. Get on board with yourself and your dream, and I assure you the right funding door will open.

Your Turn

What action steps will you take to move forward during days 1-5?

Chapter 3
Branding – Days 6-16

What is a Brand

When we talk about branding and creating a brand, most people tend to think that a brand simply means your logo. Though your logo is surely part of your brand, it is by no means the complete picture. A brand encompasses everything your business stands for. It is the personality, the principles, the values, the mission and the image of your company. Essentially, you can think of your brand as your soul's message. So what is your soul's message to the world?

How to Create Your Brand

Ultimately, brands are the preconceptions in your customers' heads. Your brand is determined by what others think when they come in contact with your brand, but that doesn't mean that you shouldn't take considerable time and effort at the outset to outline what your brand is. You want to have a clear picture of who you are and what you provide. Once you establish what your brand is at its core, you can then effectively set out to evoke those feelings and values through your logo, your font and your colors. Then, inject those values into your marketing, your content, your business practices, your customer service approach and everything else related to your business. Without this set of guideposts, however, you are literally shooting in the dark. It will be impossible to be consistent, and therefore, to create a brand that is guaranteed to provide the same, relied-upon experience - every time.

So how do you get started? What are the elements that you need to define in order to start creating your personal brand? Why can't you just start the business by getting clients and worry about the brand later?

What to Decide

First of all, get clear about what you offer. What do you do? How do you do it? For whom do you do it?

Create your 30 second elevator speech. Fill in the blanks.

My name is _____ and I help _____ struggling with _____ experience _____ as a result of working with me.

Feel free to get creative with your wording, but this is the essence of your elevator speech. Basically, when crafting your elevator speech, envision you're in an elevator with a potential customer. You have from the time the doors shut until they open to sell that person on why they should work with you as opposed to your competition. What would you say to convince him or her? What do you do differently or better or faster than everyone else?

Understand too, that your elevator speech can evolve. It doesn't have to be a set description that prevents you from growing or specializing. But create something to start and use. As you either outgrow it or your niche develops, you can always adjust and tweak your speech.

Next let's decide what your 3 Brand Values will be.

Brand Values

What do you stand for? It can be difficult to decide. It's important that your brand values are the things most important to you and not an idealized version of what you think others might want you to stand for. One trick for coming up with the values that most strike upon your core is to make a list of what you detest. This may seem counterintuitive, but it's actually an effective, efficient way to find out what makes the biggest ripple in your soul.

Try to think of your industry and a time when you were a customer in it. What bothered you the most about the experience you had? If for example, you spent time in a hospital and hated how impersonal the experience was, maybe you craft your service around the personal service that you extend to each of your clients. Maybe you were perfectly happy with the level of personal interaction, but your experience was full of sloppiness and unprofessionalism. Perhaps in your experience, nurses are always pretty personable, but it's actually more difficult to find someone who is proficient and professional; so, maybe that's the value that you showcase. Whatever it is, the value you most respect, crave and admire can often be found when you analyze what you despise.

Come up with as many as possible. Once you have this list, we'll narrow it down to the three best. Which values stand out against the rest?

These three will be your company's values. Once you know what you stand for and what values are most important to you, it will make deciding on your logo, font and other visual elements of your logo that much easier. It will also dictate the tone that you should adopt in your marketing material and make clear what the voice of your brand will be. For example, personal touch is more important to you, than you might want a logo that is softer, with warmer colors and an inviting, rounded font. But if you determine that professionalism is more important to you, you would create a logo and look that was polished, sharper and more clean. There would be no question that you were focused on the details, techniques and getting things right. You can't very well have done this in the opposite order by creating a logo that you enjoy but that doesn't speak to what you value the most. If you take this route, you will consistently be delivering something other than what you've presented to the customer, and your customer will consistently be misguided.

Guiding Principles

Now that you've established your core values, let's talk about your Guiding Principles. A simple way to think about the difference between values and principles is that your values determine your ethics and how you respond to ethical issues in your business, whereas principles determine your strategy and how you approach operating your business.

An example of a guiding principle is to "exceed customer expectations." This very well could be a guiding principle for you, whether your value is providing personable service or providing professionalism; in either case, you would act based on your principle but you might achieve something different. In the case of having "being personable" as a value, you might exceed customer expectations by sending a client a personal "thank you" or "get well" note. In the case of being professional, you might show up to your clients' house with your tools housed in a professional looking case and have the latest technology on your tablet, creating a seamless experience. Either way, once you know what your values and your principles are, every interaction and experience your clients have with you will be in accordance with your brand.

Come up with 3 Guiding Principles that will serve as the means by which your strategies and operational procedures are formed. Your guiding principles will drive your behavior in business, and your clients will come to rely on these constants when working with you.

Brand Mission

Next, you'll need to craft a mission statement for your company. Don't get overwhelmed. If you've filled in the blanks of your elevator speech, you're actually almost there. Take that sentence and add some spice.

That spice could be something like highlighting the particular values you plan to use to do what you do. It could incorporate the deeper reason behind why you've chosen to start this business. Or maybe it highlights why this industry is so important to you.

Don't be wishy- washy, or craft something that is nebulous. Think of something quantifiable so that when life and business get in the way and things get messy, you will know, without a doubt, what to do to get back to your mission statement. So use action words and use adjectives that involve the senses. Make your mission statement palpable; something that you can touch.

Get some inspiration from some of the best.

Nike: *To bring inspiration and innovation to every athlete in the world.*

Starbucks: *To inspire and nurture the human spirit – one person, one cup and one neighborhood at a time.*

Ebay: *Provide a global trading platform where practically anyone can trade practically anything.*

Patagonia: *Build the best product, cause no unnecessary harm, use business to inspire and implement solutions to the environmental crisis.*

Warby Parker: *Warby Parker was founded with a rebellious spirit and a lofty objective: to offer designer eyewear at a revolutionary price while leading the way for socially-conscious businesses.*

IKEA: *At IKEA our vision is to create a better everyday life for many people. Our business idea supports this vision by offering a wide range of well-designed, functional home furnishing products at prices so low that as many people as possible will be able to afford them.*

Honest Tea: *Honest Tea seeks to create and promote great-tasting, healthier, organic beverages. We strive to grow our business with* the same honesty and integrity we use to craft our products, with sustainability and great taste for all.

Uber: *Transportation as reliable as running water; everywhere for everyone.*

Lyft: *Providing communities with welcoming transport at affordable rates.*

Credit Karma: *We believe everyone should be empowered by their finances, not confused by them. Our goal is to continue offering valuable financial tools and resources at no cost to consumers.*

Blue Apron: *Blue Apron makes incredible home cooking accessible, for everyone.*

Be Clear and Honest

I want to bring to your attention two of the above mission statements for competitors in the same in the industry: Uber and Lyft. Notice the differences in their mission statements and what the statements tell you about each company.

Most people who use travel apps regularly know that the one main difference between using Uber versus using Lyft is that, with Lyft, you can expect a more interactive, more welcoming and friendlier ride than you can with Uber. Uber is larger and generally more upscale and professional. Pricing is similar, but when prices surge on either platform, Uber prices far exceed Lyft's prices. But being the bigger name as of right now, you can expect more immediate service from Uber. If you want a sleek, professional and always available drive, you'll go with Uber. If you want a social, interactive and less formal drive, you'll go with Lyft. You can start to see this difference in each company's mission statement. As you start to browse their apps and experience their services, this difference will make itself even more clear.

It's not important that Uber is stressing availability while Lyft is stressing affordability. There is demand for both customers, but each company is talking specifically to its target audience and making a compelling case for choosing that company. There is still plenty of business to go around for both companies. So essentially, it only benefits the company AND the customer to accurately state who your audience is. That is the point of branding: to attract and speak directly to the person who is looking for you. That's how you become of most value, so don't be afraid to spell it out to your customer.

Brand Vision

If your mission is what you hope to accomplish for your clients, your vision is more focused on understanding why you exist. So, while your mission statement should be full of action words and compelling adjectives, your vision can be more nebulous and lofty. To get at your vision, reflect back on what sparked you to start this business in the first place. What drives you? Why does your business matter to you? Your mission statement centers on what your company actually does to make money, while your vision states, essentially, why you chose to do this to earn money. Why is this the path that you want to take to supporting yourself?

It's not important that you print signs with your vision on them, or declare it on your website. You can if you choose, but your vision is the reason you come back to when you question why you're getting up to go to work every day. What's the reason beyond the service? How does doing this work fit into your larger life mission? Does this path satisfy you on a spiritual level and how do you see yourself doing God's work?

If you keep these things in mind when you're designing your logo, writing your tagline and crafting your marketing, you will strike upon the right chord and evoke the most accurate version of your business to your clients. You will create the version of your business that will leave both you and your clients fulfilled, so it is important to know and to have written, but it's not important to communicate to your client directly. If it exists and you've branded consistently, your vision will be communicated to your clients naturally and subconsciously.

Brand Personality

Now that you have the overarching values, principles, mission and vision, it's time to get into the details of your brand and to create the imagery that will become your brand's personality. Before actually creating or hiring someone to create your logo, take some time to write down the adjectives that describe your brand and company. Go big first. Write down as many as you can and then start to cross off the less important ones. Try to narrow your list down to 7 adjectives.

For example:

Is your business,

professional or personal?

serious or playful?

efficient or thorough?

Once you have your list, you can use these adjectives to help you decide on your website's colors, fonts and structure. You'll have a clearer sense of what is acceptable. If your business is quirky, then it's fine to send personable, quirky emails, but if you're trying to evoke a sense of efficient professionalism, then that's not the style email you'd want to send to clients if you want to maintain a consistent image. And you DO want to create a consistent image. When you keep showing up in someone's inbox, or in a Twitter feed, you want to have the same style message every time. It promotes a sense of trust between you and the customer. That reliability is building your brand and solidifying your image in your potential customer's mind - long before they ever pick up the phone.

Creating Your Logo

If you're not a designer, how do you go about getting started?

What we've done so far, in terms of defining the essence of your company in words, is the cornerstone of creating a logo. You could easily take a list of your top 5-7 words to a designer and have the designer create some mock-ups. Based on what your words are, it would be evident to the designer which colors would work the best, but it doesn't hurt to have a sense, going in, of what different colors symbolize. Red and yellow logos say something much different than green and blue logos. There are many resources online that can give you insight into what colors mean.

Try not to choose colors based on your personal favorites, but rather what those colors will say to your prospective client base.

Your designer will also be able to use your brand description to help decide which fonts work best in your design. Remember - different fonts serve different purposes. The font that is used in your heading is not necessarily the same font that should be used in the body of your emails or web copy. Generally, your company name might use a display or script font and your tagline might be a serif or sans serif that is easier to read.

Once your designer comes back to you with a slew of options, how do you gauge which look is the best for you business? The best comparison to use when talking about logo, colors and fonts is to think of it as the "wardrobe" your business wears. Much like you wear certain clothes to create a specific impression in different situations, your business font and colors are the first impression of your business to potential clients. You wouldn't wear sweatpants to a wedding, or a ball gown to the beach, much like you shouldn't use a whimsical font and pastel colors to advertise a service that is reliable and confident, though you might use blues and purples and a softer font to convey a sense of tranquility and relaxation.

When you settle on your logo, it's important to create a protocol for your business so that your company image is consistent. Once you know what font or fonts are in your logo, you can determine what body copy fonts best complement it. If your company name/logo is a strong, blocky typeface, that's not the font that you will use in all of your text, but you do want something that works well with it. There aren't rules on what does or doesn't work, but if it's sending the wrong message, or if it looks too busy, than it's not the right fit. Whatever you decide, stick to the standards that you set out for your business and make sure that all of your marketing materials maintain a consistent look. You might even want to create a folder, either on your computer or in an actual filing cabinet, where you record what your "official" business fonts are and what the hexadecimals of your colors are. If you don't know, a hexadecimal is the number/letter code that designers use to identify colors. This way you're not guessing at which shade of green your logo is - you know the exact color.

Your Turn

What action steps will you take to move forward during days 6-16?

Chapter 4
Getting Ready/Envisioning Your Schedule – Days 17-24

It's important at this point, now that you've taken some time to determine your company structure, define your company's mission and articulate the essence of your brand, to step back for a moment and envision how you want the overall workings of your life to play out as you move forward.

Your Plan

In this chapter, we are going to envision and create your plan, but not your business plan. Creating a business plan at this point would mean getting mired in details before we have a complete picture of where we wish to end up. Right now, we are more concerned with your exit strategy from your current lifestyle. In order to know where you hope to end up, it's helpful to take stock of where you currently are, what you'd like to see different and how to recognize success when it comes.

Most people get stuck around this point of starting their own business because they don't see a clear passage or transition that can take them from where they are now to where they want to be. It may all sound really great - this brand name, logo and concept - but how does it transform from concept to real business? Funds, clients and paychecks surely won't come just because you've incorporated your business. After all - you're in your current job for a reason. It pays the bills, and without it, you'd have no way to pay your expenses, raise your family and support yourself.

That's why we're going to create both an exit strategy and a vision of the future, so that you can follow the strategy until you can permanently shut the door on your old life and enter into the future you've dreamed for yourself.

Take a moment to answer these questions

From a financial standpoint, how much or little to you need to work at your current job in order to make ends meet while you transition into starting your own business?

How does your schedule look right now, and how would it look it you were to work only part time, as-needed, or not at all (depending on what you answered above)? What does the day look like from sun up to sun down? How much time would you have in your schedule? Do you have other commitments during the day that you need to include (picking kids up from school, taking care of family members, etc.)?

How do you envision your physical health being affected as you transition from the schedule you have now to the schedule you dream of?

How do you envision your spiritual health being affected as you transition from the schedule you have now to the schedule you dream of?

How do you envision your financial health being affected as you transition from the schedule you have now to the schedule you dream of?

Create a budget with your current income, and describe how you plan to save for the final exit from your current position.

Create a schedule for yourself that denotes how much time you can dedicate to your business around your current job schedule.

How does your dream schedule look? How is your time spent once you are running your own business?

If self-employment is the path for you, I'm sure that your description of what you've envisioned in your dream scenario is much more satisfying and fulfilling than what your current reality is. Therefore, the description of what you've written is what success looks like for you. So you will know if you've achieved success by whether your physical, spiritual and financial health are in accordance with what you've envisioned. By simply identifying what success looks like, not only have you increased your chances of attaining it, but you've also created a guide that you can refer back to from time to time. If, down the line, you're stressed financially, you'll know that you're not making enough money, and that you need to find more clients or spend more time marketing in order to find balance. Similarly, if you are physically tired, maybe you've taken on too many clients, or need to hire an assistant to help out.

Remember - the end goal is to create a life for yourself that is more balanced and healthier than the one in which you're currently entrenched. By working for yourself, you'll have the control to run the business as you want, and you'll know best how to do that based on how you feel physically, spiritually and financially. If one of those areas is out of balance, you'll need to recalibrate. What you've just created is a great guidepost, because, especially early on, you will be working a lot to develop traction and get the business going, but if you don't know what you're working toward, you could spend forever grinding gears without realizing when to ease up.

What is the Exit Plan?

So, you've determined how much you currently need to work in order to support yourself and your family, and, based on that, you've also planned how much time you have leftover to dedicate to this new business. Based on those two figures, you should also have an idea of how long you need to continue in your current job before you can totally transition out.

Many people find the most challenging part of the transition to be the risk of complacency. Whenever you have one foot in and one foot out of something, there is a risk of inaction. In the transitional phase, you still have the relative comfort of the steady paycheck, and you feel like you're working on your business, but because you have that safety net, there is little compelling force motivating you to continue pulling away from that net. The final step of leaving your job for good is going to be a leap. That's why you need to set a date. It's like ripping off a Band-Aid. It's so much easier to just leave it on and let it fall off on its own, but that's not how things happen. You have to take the action!

This human tendency toward complacency is the same reason why, sometimes, people take that sudden leap, even when they're not ready...because it lights some proverbial fire beneath them and will motivate them by sheer panic. There's some credence to this tactic, and I'd say it depends a great deal on your circumstances. If, for example, you don't have many assets, or a family, and you have a hefty savings account, then maybe this tactic would work for you. But if the weight of your life and responsibilities require tending, then you'll need your current income, or a portion of it, to assist in your transition.

Generally, though, the best technique is to set an imaginary fire beneath you. So keep your job, but set in your mind a firm date of exit. Make the date non-negotiable. In your head, you can tell yourself that your job is gone as of this date. There is no turning back. Either you have your own business up and running...or that's it. You're done. Automate a predetermined allocation of money to go into a savings account, so that you're not relying on yourself to put away the money that you need. Take that responsibility off your shoulders. And force yourself to work on the business. If you have a half hour a day, or four hours on the weekend, or if you have to get up an hour earlier every day, carve out the time. Your business isn't going to materialize because you envisioned it. You can trust it will look like what you envision if you take the time to work on it, but that won't happen without your attention and legwork.

How Much Can You Stand to Lose? Risk.

Something that's not often talked about, but that is a valuable limit to know, is how much you can stand to lose. Not every business is a success. Not every idea a business tries is a success. Not every successful business is successful right away. So, it's important to know where you stand with risk.

For example, a restaurant may try opening for breakfast in addition to lunch and dinner. Obviously, unless they put in massive marketing efforts to start, it will take some time before the community learns that the restaurant is open for breakfast. Going into this endeavor, the business should already have an idea of how long they will maintain these new hours, regardless of whether they are earning a profit or not. They have to assume a learning curve; but they must also know how long they are willing to try the new hours before bailing out. So, if they know they can operate for three months at a loss, and are willing to risk it based on the possibility for increased sales once the new hours are common knowledge, they can plan to go full force for those three months. This way, they don't risk giving up too soon. If they give up after the second month, out of fear, and don't trust in the risk they are taking, they may have missed out on what was a good opportunity that simply took time to gain traction. Similarly, they can't go on forever operating at a loss just because they want to serve breakfast.

The same is true for you. It's not a bad omen, or a jinx, to define your "deal-breaker" results. Determine a realistic time frame to dedicate to this endeavor whole-heartedly, and if it's not working after a certain point, allow yourself to opt out or to simply refocus. It could be that, if you are not hitting your goals, you simply need to realign with your mission or redefine your niche. Maybe there is one small element that, if tweaked, would make all the difference. Like, maybe your target audience is off or maybe you're not marketing where your target audience is looking. We'll address these details more later on, but for now, the important thing to note is that it's important to know where your limits are and stick to them.

What, when you see it, will tell you that it's time to take a closer look and readjust? Write it down because it's important to know, but then get it out of your head and focus on success.

Your Turn

What action steps will you take to move forward during days 17-24?

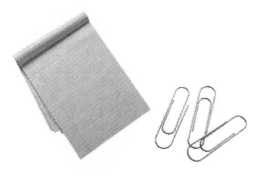

Chapter 5
Business Plan – Days 25-39

We've covered parts of what your business plan will include when we talked about your mission and principles. And we've established a little bit about the structure of the business. But now it's time to get the entire plan on paper. Don't be intimidated by the business plan. It's simply a guidepost for you to follow so that you can have a clear company direction, and its existence will streamline your efforts. It's also necessary to have if you plan on seeking funding. Your business plan is the map to your success.

What Are You Selling?

The first question is, "What are you selling?" The answer might appear to be straightforward and obvious, but what are you really selling? You want to not only know what product or service you're offering, but what people are actually buying when they purchase it. What problem are you solving for your customer?

For example, when someone purchases a weight loss DVD, yes...they are literally buying a DVD, but the real investment is in the hope of a brighter future, the future where they're fit and thin and healthy. They are buying the dream, and that's what you're actually selling.

One way to easily break this down is by making a list of all the features of your product or service, such as convenience, reliability, experience, prompt service, personal service, etc.

Then make a list of what benefits those features actually provide to your customer. If we were selling a cup of coffee, the features might be hot and fresh and fast. But the actual benefits a customer receives when they get their coffee hot, fresh and fast is that they get a great-tasting pick-me-up without being late for school drop off. If you're a customer who's not interested in getting to your destination quickly, and you prefer a gourmet roast or are more concerned with free refills or the cheapest coffee, then maybe you'd select a different coffee shop. But for anyone who wants something that tastes good on the go, this shop is a no-brainer.

Your business is the same way. You provide something specific that means a clear outcome for your customer. What is it?

Knowing the features and benefits of your product or service is going to help you understand where you fit in your industry and to understand your target market and your demographic. This leads us to our next question.

Who is Your Ideal Customer?

And don't say anyone is your ideal customer because you can help anyone in need. That's not true (from a business standpoint, anyway). Even if your ideal customer was anyone in need, that's actually a very specific customer. That would mean your ideal customer was the one who had no time to be selective, that you were always on call, first to the scene and you'd structure your business accordingly.

But right now, as you create this business, your job is to uncover and describe who your ideal customer is. Is it people of a certain age, with a certain ailment, in a certain situation? Knowing exactly who your customer is will not only help you in your marketing, by determining what kind of language you use, it will help you with your overall plan. Once you know who your customer is, you'll be able to get a better sense of what makes them act. You can determine how they shop. Do they look online for advice, or seek out referrals? Are they cautious and thorough when making decisions, or are they impulsive? You'll also be able to determine where they're located and how you can reach them.

But if you don't to whom you're talking and for whom you are looking, you'll never be able to reach them. If you try to speak to everyone and anyone, you'll end up affecting no one. So get specific. It might help to draw or create actual personas or descriptions. Envision your ideal customer as someone you know, whether in real life or from a novel. If you can picture them, you'll naturally be more able to market and help them.

Also, when it comes to your ideal customer, how big is this market? Is it a substantial part of the population? Does this customer live in your area? If your business is providing a service, you will naturally have to be accessible. This is less important if you're selling a product, since you can ship anything anywhere. How receptive is your ideal customer to the different forms of marketing? If your niche is focused on geriatric medicine, it wouldn't be prudent to concentrate your marketing efforts online...unless, of course, you determine that the actual buyer of your services are the children of older individuals. If that were the case, it'd mean your ideal customer is actually not an elderly person at all, but a person likely to have an elderly parent. These differentiations are important to learn and fine tune.

Let's rewind for a moment. When you were describing what you really sell earlier, you might've said something like, "reliable-home care for the elderly." But that's not what you provide. What you're really providing might be, "peace of mind for adults struggling with an ailing parent." This means that your *ideal patient* is older in age, but it would also mean that your *ideal customer* is someone, probably with kids and a spouse, but who is the primary person responsible for caring for an aging parent. You would talk to this person much differently than you would to the patient, and therefore, your entire business strategy should reflect that.

Who's on Your Team

Will your business be just you, or will it include others? If it's just you, that's perfectly fine. Do you want it to always be just you, or do you hope to grow to the point where you can hire others? Are you starting this venture with one or more founders? If so, take a moment to assess how your skills match up and whether or not they complement each other's skills. Ideally, you don't want a partner with the same skill set as you. It will be to your advantage if you can pair or group different strengths that are important in your industry. What you DO want to have in common with any founding team member is core values. Do you share the same goals and core beliefs? If these things are in line, then you'll probably be able to resolve any differences that come up along the way.

Who's Your Competition

It's important to know your competition. What other products or services already exist in your market? Research your competition and find out what they offer, how they provide it and how and where they advertise. It's wise to be informed. And in fact, the key to your unique value proposition could be held in what your competition ISN'T doing.

The more informed you are about all of your competition, the more successful and prepared you will be. You don't want to know what they're doing so that you can imitate them. You want to know what they're doing so that you can find out what they're missing or who they're NOT targeting. That could be your niche.

Also, make sure to look at your competition comprehensively. By this I mean looking at all the variations of offerings that are competitive with your product or service. For example, say a convenience store starts offering pizza slices. At first glance, you might think that their competition is all the local pizzerias, but that's actually not the case. The convenience store isn't offering pizza to compete with Uncle Tony's authentic pizzeria. The person who goes to Uncle Tony's wants an authentic slice of pie, and isn't concerned about price or convenience. The real competition for the convenience store is all the other quick service food retailers who serve something quick and cheap for lunch. The convenience store competes more directly with the fast food restaurants than with the other pizza parlors in the area. Their goal is to find the customers who need a quick, cheap meal and persuade him/her that their pizza is the answer. It is NOT to find the customer who is looking for pizza and convince them that their slice is the best. This understanding determines their entire marketing approach.

In other words, your competition could be in places you don't immediately suspect. Think of the people who need your service. If you aren't there, what are their other options? How do they solve their problem? Take a look at your answers. The companies that provide the things you listed are your competition. Even if their solutions are not the same service or product you provide, if it's solving the problem that your ideal customer has, they are your competition. So, how do you compete with them?

Financials

The financial section of your business plan is critical if you plan on seeking investors or obtaining a bank loan, but it's equally important even if you don't require funding; your financials are an unbiased means to steer the business. Essentially, you are creating your best guess as to the financial outlook of your business into the future. You do this by combining your projected costs, expenses and taxes with your projected profits.

There are much more detailed resources out there regarding exactly what to include and how to calculate the numbers, but what I'll get into here is why it's important. Basically, you want to know what your projected expenses and earnings are so that you can make informed decisions about where to spend your money, how much to market, when to hire additional employees and so on.

It's tempting to think that if you can find x number of clients, they'll pay x amount of dollars, and that some of the money will go to expenses and the rest will be profit. But it's not that simple.

Whether you are selling a product or a service, there are multiple expenses that go along with providing that product or service. If you're providing a service, you need to travel to the client, you likely need to be insured, you need supplies, there might be licensing fees and applicable taxes...the list goes on. If you have a product, there will be costs for packaging, storage, fulfillment, design, inventory tracking and shipping.

Additionally, you will need to consider cash flow. If you are invoicing people, there will be a lag between the time you invoice and the time the money enters your account. How will you set up your business so that there is a healthy cash flow?

It's only through sitting down and devising projections that you can accurately come up with a pricing structure for your product or services that makes sense for both you and the client.

How Will You Market?

Once you have your financials completed, you will be able to see how much you can afford to spend on marketing. Once you know that number, you can decide what forms of marketing make the most sense for you.

Remember - this doesn't have to stay the same every year. You can try different marketing avenues and track what works and what doesn't.

It's usually best to spread out your marketing efforts across a few different channels. You don't want to drop all of your money into one basket unless, of course, you think it makes sense to do so. Here is where you'll really want to get into the mind of your ideal customer. To what do they pay attention, and how can you get their attention?

Especially with the prevalence of the Internet, there are many avenues that are free, or low cost, so you can work around high priced alternatives by supplementing with free marketing. We'll go into more detail about marketing online in the next chapter, but for now, start to get an idea of where your customers are and what would be the best channels in which you should advertise.

Aside from the conventional marketing channels, there's one that I want to mention because it's not particularly well-known, but I've found it to be effective and targeted. These days, millions of podcasts exist on nearly any topic you can think of. Many of those podcasts are put online for free, or mostly at the expense of the podcasters themselves, so often you'll hear a podcast host take a break to mention a sponsor. If you've deemed your target audience as those that would listen to a podcast on a specific topic, seek out those podcasts and see if you could sponsor a few episodes of the podcast. I love the idea of advertising this way, because it's such a great transaction. You're donating directly to the people who need funds to continue creating the content to which you're listening, so it feels like a better use of money than what you spend for an ad in the paper or for a regular radio ad. And you're talking directly into the ear of someone who might find your services valuable. It's a win-win.

What Does the Future Look Like?

You'll want to include in your business plan where you see your business 1, 3 and 5 years down the line. It's easiest to start big and decide what you want your business to look like in 5 years. How busy do you want to be? How much do you want to be earning? That will determine how many clients you need, per week, in order to maintain that figure. Or is your goal different – perhaps, at 5 years, you hope to have removed yourself as primary operator and have others who you manage? If that's the case, you still need to know how much you're making; but also...what does it cost to employ the individuals that you will oversee? What role do you then play?

Remember that this is your dream and vision, so your plan is up to you. There's no need to set stringent limits on what you can achieve, or stick to conventional patterns. If it's somewhere you can be, realistically, in 5 years, sketch it out. From here we're working backwards, so based on what you see in your 5-year plan, we'll have a better idea of what needs to be in place in your 3-year plan.

In order for your 5-year plan to come to fruition, your business has to be making money by your third year. So, what will it take for you to be making money in your third year? What is in the early stages at 3 years, that's full grown, at 5 years?

Depending on what your 3-year plan looks like, what does that mean for your 1-year plan? Where do you see yourself 1 year from today? How many clients do you need to have at the 1-year mark to ensure that you're on the right trajectory?

Once you have an idea of what you want your business to look like at these milestones, it will be clear what daily steps you need to be taking in order to hit these goals.

Also, make sure to occasionally revisit these plans so that you can be sure that you're moving at the right pace and staying on track.

Also remember that these plans don't need to be stagnant documents. They are a living business plan, so if your goals change, you can feel free to adjust the plan. It makes no sense to have a 5-year plan that no longer fits with your mission. At this point in the game, you actually know where the business is going to take you. New doors might open, hidden niches might appear, and by-passed demographics might surface. You might see an opportunity that you couldn't have imagined when you started, but are suddenly positioned to do something about. You want to leave room for this sort of thing. Your plans don't need to be set in stone. They're just paper, a place to start. As you continue to revisit your plans moving forward, edit and adjust so that you always have a clear destination in mind. You might not get to the exact destination you sketch out, but you'll find that when you stay aware, you'll get to the destination where you're meant to go.

Dedicate time to periodically reconnect with your purpose. It is at these points that you can assess where you stand on an emotional, physical, mental and spiritual level. How can you edit your plan so that your core self is consistently in balance?

Do a SWOT Analysis

SWOT stands for: Strengths, Weaknesses, Opportunities and Threats

You can do a SWOT analysis for any business decision you make, but it is an especially great asset, when you're starting your business, in order to get a sense of the entire industry picture. It's important to look at these four categories from an unbiased perspective, as it can be tempting to gloss over what is unpleasant or what is not exciting. However, recognizing weaknesses and threats is a lot different than expecting them. In the analysis, we simply want to be aware of both what makes the business a strong venture and what potential weaknesses exist so that we can figure out solutions and alternatives now before we dig deeper.

The easiest way to do a SWOT analysis on your business is to draw four columns and then to go through each one thoroughly.

Strengths

Here list everything your business will thrive at. You can list all the good things it will do, the ways in which it will help people, or save them money. List why the niche you've chosen is perfectly suited to your region, or how many ideal customers are clustered in the area. List whatever you can think of.

Weaknesses

Now list everything with which your business will struggle. Maybe you do not have large funds to dedicate to marketing, or maybe you don't live in an area with many people, so it might be difficult to find clients. Maybe you live in an area with a lot of competition. Maybe you are unsure if people will recognize that they need your service and you might have to educate them first on what you even offer.

Opportunities

These are circumstances that your business is positioned to take advantage of. Perhaps there is an upcoming healthcare law that would make your service extra coveted, or maybe a nearby hospital is closing and you can make use of that situation to get clients.

Threats

These are the circumstances by which your business is positioned to be hurt. Maybe there are certain laws or restrictions coming soon that will make it harder for your target audience to use you, or maybe a new facility is moving to your neighborhood that could make your services less coveted.

Once you have completed this list, you now will have a sense of where to focus energy and resources and where you might need to readjust, based on what's coming. If a new nursing facility is opening up down the street, how can you reorganize your image so that you are solving a problem for people that the facility is not? Are there marketing or operational changes that you need to make in order to stay ahead of the curve? Hopefully, you will see what these things are, once you have done your SWOT analysis, and you will be better equipped to deal with both the negative and positive elements that might arise.

Insurance & Accounting
Insurance

As a self-employed nurse entrepreneur, you will definitely need to have insurance. Even the best nurses are at risk of being sued for malpractice or negligence. It has less to do with your ability than it does with the society in which we live and the chance that something out of your control can so easily happen while you're caring for a patient. All it takes to get sued is for your client to "perceive" negligence. It's impossible to anticipate every outcome, so even the most meticulous practitioners still encounter situations in which they are blamed for unanticipated outcomes. Allergies or sudden accidents can be perceived as the fault of the clinician. Therefore, insurance is a must. Professional Liability Insurance will protect you in these cases. Your business is as much your asset as your car or your house. You would insure these things, so you must also insure your business. Rates for a generous policy should be more affordable than you might imagine.

Let me mention here that, at this time, you might want to obtain a lawyer or legal counsel on your team as well. The peace of mind is well worth it.

Accounting

Accounting is important all year long, but it perhaps never feels more important than during tax season. Doing the taxes for your business will be lot more pleasant if you keep up with your accounting tasks on a regular basis. The easiest option is to consult with an accountant at the outset. He/she can set up simple systems that you can follow all year long so that you are not scrambling to find receipts and invoices when you sit down to do your taxes. The best advice when you are first starting out is to keep excellent records. When you do your taxes (if you do them yourself), you'll get a firsthand sense of what you can deduct and what's important to have a record of. So it will help if, during the year, you keep records of all of your expenses in one place. If you're not sure whether or not you'll need something, save it anyway. It will be better to have more information than not enough.

Things will get more complicated if you're selling physical products for which you have an inventory. In that case, I'd seek the consult of an accountant to help determine how you should be tracking inventory and related expenses.

Programs, like Quickbooks, can also be a lifesaver and are fairly user-friendly. Quickbooks is related to Turbotax, which will make doing your taxes a bit easier. If you're on a budget, you might even be able to solicit the help of an accounting-savvy friend. You can barter services if it works.

Your Turn

What action steps will you take to move forward during days 25-39?

Chapter 6
Marketing – Days 40-53

Have a Plan

When it comes to marketing, you must start with a plan. Trust me - marketing can turn into a black hole that you just toss money into if you don't go in with a strategy. There are so many marketing opportunities available these days, and any of them sounds like the next greatest idea, but not all are right for your business and for talking to YOUR client. That's why it's imperative to create a marketing plan, both when you're first starting your business and at the start of every year.

Your first marketing plan is going to be a lot of guessing. You're going to try things, and if they don't provide the desired results, that just means it's time to adjust your plan. As you try different marketing tactics and measure the results, you'll have more to go on as you move forward. Starting out, it will be all trial and error. The important part is that you have a plan from which to start and that you continuously measure your results; this will go a long way in helping you to shape a future that you desire.

If you can answer these three questions, you'll have the framework for all that comes after. Without these answers, you're literally going to be shooting in the dark. We've touched on these concepts in previous chapters, but these are things that are imperative to know when setting up your marketing plan.

1. A clear, focused reason as to why your customer will use you. We've been through this before, but what is the core reason that a customer specifically needs your services? Is it because you are so efficient? Are you more attentive, always available, an expert in one particular area?

2. Who is your target customer? Now that you know what exactly you provide, determine who the person is who needs exactly that. Write a description of that person, their likes, dislikes, age, circumstances, gender, location, etc. It might help to give this person a name. Have them in mind whenever you're creating marketing materials. Be authentic and this will resonate with your audience.

3. When it comes to this target audience, what other competitors are vying for their attention? There is always another way your target audience can spend their money. There's always another service or product that they might purchase instead. Take the time to find out what these are in your industry so that you can adapt your marketing efforts to be the better solution. Just remember that it's impossible to be better if you don't know what your competition is doing.

All of these answers come together to form your tagline, or USP (unique selling proposition). It's basically a concise version of your elevator speech. But from here, we can start to get a sense of where to focus your marketing efforts.

Determine Your Marketing Goals

It's difficult to know if your marketing dollars are working unless you have specific marketing goals or objectives. In your first year, this might be something like getting enough customers to be able to support yourself full-time. Maybe you already have a handful of customers, but they aren't ideal, whether it's because they are located far away or schedule too sporadically. In that case, maybe your objective will to be to increase revenue by acquiring higher quality leads. Either way, determine what it is that you need your marketing to achieve. The more specific you can be, the better.

The How and What

Once you know what you want to achieve, it's time to come up with the "How" (i.e. your strategy), and the "What" (i.e. your tactics). Your strategy is going to echo your USP a bit. It's the, "**How** are you going to generate revenue?" It will be the unique way in which you plan on enticing more customers to you. So, maybe your strategy is to "Always give a little bit more," or to "Go above and beyond." With this overarching strategy in mind, you can begin to form tactics. What are the actual things that you will do that will ensure that you're going above and beyond? Maybe you offer payment plans, or you visit a client's house at odd hours, or you send text messages reminding clients to take their meds or do their physical therapy exercises. Whatever they are, tactics should coincide with and reinforce your strategy.

This is helpful, too, in knowing where NOT to focus your efforts. If you get a sales call from a coupon company suggesting you do a coupon with them, you can refer back to your strategy. Does offering a coupon fit in with "going above and beyond?" Not really? Maybe if you were attempting to generate revenue this year by providing extra value, it would make sense, but since it doesn't fit in with your current strategy, you can table that idea for another year when maybe you have a different strategy. This is a great way to separate what marketing opportunities to take advantage of and which to pass on. So, stay consistent, stay on theme and find success.

Website & Logo

We talked about creating a logo earlier, so you may already have that completed. Now it's time to take your logo and use it in the creation of your website. When it comes to creating your website, you have two choices. You can either hire a graphic designer and/or a copywriter to do it for you. This can be costly, but many would say that it's well worth it. A designer will be able to construct the entire site for you and determine the layout. A copywriter will provide the copy and generally will be able to SEO optimize the copy so that your site is getting indexed by Google.

The second option is to create your website yourself. There are many resources online these days that don't require that you know any HTML coding in order to create your own website. WordPress and Squarespace are two popular choices, if you want to take the website creation into your own hands.

Either way you go, you want to make sure that the final version of your website is consistent with your brand, your mission and your vision. You want the language, the fonts, the colors and the photos to all reinforce who and what your company is.

Your site should be straightforward and easy to navigate. A prospective client shouldn't have to go far to understand what it is you provide and how to hire you. Whether you're doing it yourself, or hiring someone to do your site for you, take some time to Google great websites, both in and outside of your industry, to see what works and what doesn't. Take notes on what you do or don't like from the sites and either pass them along to your designer or integrate these into your own design.

Social Media

Once you've established your marketing strategy, determined your target audience and have a website, you can start to develop your social media presence. Start with what's manageable for you. It's fine to start small. You don't have to create accounts on every platform at once. Choose one or two that you can develop and do well, and then you can gradually expand to other platforms. You'll want to determine where, on social media, most of your target customers spend their time and choose that platform as your starting point. Once your social media channels are up and running, you'll want to make sure to connect them to your website. Customers should be able to easily get from your website to your social media sites and from your social media sites to your website.

As you start to put your business onto social media, it's important to remember to stay consistent with your handle name. Your "handle" is your personalized URL on any given platform. So, if your business name is *Nancy's Nursing*, you'll want to make your handle is something like *Nancy's Nursing* on every platform.

Avoid being *"Nancy the Nurse"* on Facebook and *"NNursing"* on Twitter and *"NurseNancy"* on Instagram. Using different versions of your name is confusing for your customer. You want to build your brand by always being one thing, whatever that one thing is. Once you settle on what works best with your brand, use that handle consistently through everything.

You'll also want to make sure that your social media photo is a clear, high resolution version of your logo and that it's appropriately spaced so it's not cut out of the available space. Some platforms, like Facebook and Twitter, also allow you to have a cover photo, which you can change periodically based on your current promotions, the seasons and upcoming events you're attending. I'll discuss a great and easy place to do your photo editing later - without having to learn Photoshop.

Facebook

Starting a business page on Facebook is easy to do. All you need is to have an existing personal account to get started. If you don't already have one, it's easy to create. From there, you can create a page dedicated to your business. You can invite your friends to like and share your page, and then customers will be able to find your page either organically or through paid advertising. There are ways within Facebook to promote your posts and to target them to specific demographics. Plus, you can also buy advertising, outside of Facebook, that will direct viewers back to your Facebook page.

Facebook is great because you can post plain text, pictures, videos or blogs. Usually, posts with images generate more engagement than words, and videos (short clips and gifs) get even more engagement than images. You can intersperse all of these on your page. Facebook is a great way to make announcements, and promote special deals, to your followers. You can even create specific pages for events that you are holding.

Twitter

Twitter is another great social media channel. You don't need a personal account on Twitter to start a business page. Simply create your username and fill out your profile with a short version of your elevator speech, and you're good to go.

Twitter is real time, so your tweets are coming and going very quickly. Also, you can see, to the left of your screen, what hashtags are trending. If you can find a way to make them applicable to your business, you can use these to quickly jump into a bigger conversation.

Wait, What Are Hashtags?!

Hashtags are basically a way of sorting information on various social media platforms. They make it easy to participate and comment on specific instances and situations. You might see #HealthyLiving after a post that offers tips on health advice. Often on Thursdays, you'll see #ThrowbackThursday trending on the side of the screen. For some companies, this a great opportunity to post a picture of their brand from years ago and hashtag it #ThrowbackThursday.

Instagram

Instagram is photo-centric social media platform. You might find that this is a good choice for your business. Currently, Instagram is app based, which means you'll have to access it from your phone. You can see your posts on your computer, but the only way to post new images is to do so on your phone. If your business is nutrition-based, for example, Instagram might be a great place for you to post pictures of healthy recipes for your followers. Instagram is also hashtag-friendly and what's trending on Twitter might also be trending here.

LinkedIn

The crowd on LinkedIn is more business-savvy than those on other social media platforms. It's a great place to post industry articles. If your business is geared toward helping your clients navigate health insurance, or maybe on selling medical supplies, LinkedIn might be a good place to show off your expertise in the industry. Also, if you ever require employees, LinkedIn is a great place to post employment opportunities.

YouTube

You can get really creative on YouTube. Maybe your business is focused on house calls, but a great way to build your reputation and showcase your knowledge could be for you to start a YouTube channel where you have videos showing how to deal with common household accidents. Maybe you record videos showing people how to properly wash a cut, or what to do when you sprain your ankle. By providing people with all of these free tips, when something more serious occurs, your name will be the first one that comes to mind.

Hootsuite

Once you get yourself set up on the number of social media platforms that are right for you, it's time to automate. Hootsuite is a great place to do this. It's free and it supports multiple platforms. It's basically one screen where you can see all of your social media posts and comments. Also (and most importantly), from here you can schedule posts ahead of time. This is helpful because it means you can take time on one day to create posts for the entire week, then you can schedule individual posts to go out each day at a certain time and on each social network. You can experiment with what times work best to post on whichever social networks in your industry. There's a lot of existing research out there that will tell you the best times to post for maximum readership.

One of the great things about Hootsuite is that it saves you from logging onto each network and getting caught up in the social media vortex. Oftentimes, simply logging onto social media can wind up turning into a multiple hour endeavor. You'll want to respond to any comments that your posts receive, and you'll be able to see all of these interactions from your Hootsuite dashboard. But, especially in these early days of building your business, you definitely don't want to risk losing hours to endless scrolling. So, in this sense, Hootsuite is a lifesaver.

Keep in mind, however, that Twitter, Facebook and Instagram have different formats in which your posts appear, so you'll want to create your content specifically formatted to look best on each site. That's where Canva comes in.

Canva

Canva is an easy-to use, photo-editing site where you can create great looking images for your posts. They also have simple, pre-sized templates labeled for every social media channel, blog post sizing and more. Canva is free to use, but they also have a business membership, which allows you to create templates using your business colors, save logos and magically resize your art for multiple platforms at once. Feel free to experiment and see if it's a worthwhile investment for you.

Email Marketing

Email marketing is a great way to build and market to your audience. You can easily create a opt-in for a freebie on your website to collect emails. You can format this as a sign up to your monthly newsletter or as an "enter your email to receive a free tip sheet." Once you start collecting emails, you can keep in touch with your list through periodic email marketing. Your email marketing doesn't have to always be sales-focused and promotional. You can simply keep in touch with your members by sending a newsletter full of helpful advice.

Constant Contact and Mail Chimp are two great email marketing services. Both have lots of versatility and can be used to send very professional looking emails to your lists. They both offer easy-to-use templates and different automation options.

Take advantage of holidays and current events to talk to your audience; also think about your market and what their lives look like. If you work with a lot of mothers, you can use the start of the school year to offer services or tips on staying healthy in a germ-filled classroom. The most important things to remember are to be relevant, interesting and authentic. If your emails are all of those things, people will look forward to hearing from you rather than seeing your emails as pushy and overly promotional.

Podcasts

Podcasts are another great way to share content. One of the great things about podcasts is that they are so easy to consume. They can be listened to on nearly any device and listened to anywhere, from the commute to work, a walk around the park or cleaning the house. If you're a podcast consumer, I'm sure you already know the versatility of this listening medium and the variety of topics that podcasts can cover.

So, it's quite possible that a podcast can make sense for your business. For example, if you work with customers to navigate the health insurance process, a podcast on health care could be a great choice. Remember - the point of your podcast is not to sell anything directly; it's simply to present yourself as an expert in your field and create a rapport with listeners so that down the road, when they have a need, they will already trust you and want to do business with you.

Business Cards

Business cards are another important element of your business. Your business card is a mini projection of your overall business, so the image it presents should be reflective of your business as a whole. If you make a terribly generic or cluttered card, then that's what people will associate with your business. There are plenty of places online where you can make a professional looking card for a very economical price.

Your business card is also going to be the easiest bit of advertising you create, especially if you offer regional services, as you can put your business card in every bill and piece of mail that you send out. It's essentially free and you're getting the word out. After all, the person working at your oil company may one day require your services, so why not be the first name that comes to mind?

You'll also want to carry a handful of business cards wherever you go. You never know when you'll talk to someone who is interested in your services. The last thing that you want to do when you have a personal connection like that is to say that you've forgotten all of your cards at home.

Also, when creating your business card, try to think if there is something relevant to your company that you can put on the card that would make a person want to hang onto it. Maybe a quick reference of three kinds of coughs and what type of cough medicine is best for each, or maybe you alternate between a few different images on the front, each with a health tip of some sort. Don't be afraid to be creative as long as it's relevant, consistent with your image and doesn't clutter the card. You still want all the relevant information easy to read.

Marketing Brochures

A simple trifold brochure is all I would really recommend for printed marketing materials, beyond the business card. A simple brochure should basically be a foldable version of your website. On the front panel, your business name and tagline will do. Inside, include your services, the benefits of working with you, some testimonials and your contact information.

Brochures are an easy thing to leave at local businesses, schools, libraries and grocery stores. A brochure is also a nice reference material to leave with your client after the first visit. It looks professional and is a physical reminder of how to get in contact with you to reschedule.   scan code &
                                                                                                                        app

Professional Photos

Take the time to get professional business photos for your website and LinkedIn page. Nothing is more unprofessional than to see what was clearly a snapshot of you and a friend on vacation cropped so that you're the only one in the photo. It's definitely worth it to invest a few dollars into getting some professional shots. These will also come in handy down the line if and when you decide to do live events or write ebooks, as you'll need a clear, crisp image of yourself for these things, as well.

If money is an issue at the outset, don't rule out working with local photography students or bartering your services with local photographers.

Networking Events

Networking events are the perfect opportunity to get your name out into the community. For some, the thought of attending networking events is horrifying, whereas for others, it sounds like a refreshing break after all of this sitting-behind-a-computer marketing. It doesn't have to be intimidating, though. There are many Meetup groups and smaller events that you can find that are geared toward networking in relaxing settings. It's not always as official as a Chamber of Commerce meeting.

You can find periodic local events where, over breakfast, speakers talk about small business and entrepreneurship, or "meet and greets" after work at a bar. The most important thing is to just be you. Make sure you have your elevator speech committed to memory because you'll be reciting it nearly every time you shake a hand, and you'll most likely be handing out a plethora of business cards.

What's great about networking events is that they are a chance to meet people face to face, which immediately sets you apart from the scores of online people in your industry. Whether someone needs you immediately or not, you've instantly gained a measure of rapport that would take numerous interactions to achieve online. As social creatures, humans are more apt to choose to work with a person whom they've met rather than with someone who is simply a name online. In reality, they don't know you any better, but there is something to be said for having shaken hands with a person and exchanged a few words. It goes a long way.

Relationship Building

Ultimately, nurturing and growing a business is all about relationship building. Whether you're doing it online or in person, customers will continue to be your customers because of the relationships you've established with them. Most often, the companies that you abandon are the ones who've done something wrong in the relationship department. Perhaps you were overcharged or treated poorly, or the service you received was sub-par. Whatever the case, your relationship suffered, and you turned elsewhere to satisfy whatever need they were not filling.

The same is true for your business. The healthier the business relationships you have and maintain, the more return clients you'll have. It helps to embody the Golden Rule and to treat your customers as you wish to be treated. Anyone can get lucky and secure a client once, but without nurturing the relationship, you're not likely to see that client again. Additionally, happy clients tell people about their good experiences. This is the best sort of advertising.

Though remember...as often as happy clients talk, unhappy clients shout, and they do so even more often than their happy counterparts. So, relationship building is very much about handling the miscommunications and disappointments, as well.

Especially with social media as such an easy way for unhappy customers to vent, you might find that clients talk the most when something goes wrong. Never back away from this sort of talk. To attack, argue or disregard a negative comment will make you look guilty. Respond to negative feedback calmly, honestly and apologetically. Listen first. Nine times out of ten, the client just wanted to be heard, and their response will usually be conciliatory. This will also show people who are reading the comments that you're listening and willing to resolve the issue. It's a visual demonstration of how they will be treated should they work with you. Though don't show all your cards. Apologize, admit that the negative experience was unusual and unacceptable and then take it to a private or direct message if you plan to offer some consolation discount or refund. You don't want people complaining simply to receive free services, but you do want them to know that you're willing to do what it takes to keep your customers happy.

You also never know from where eventual customers may come. So, always be networking, whether you're at your child's baseball game, the grocery store or a dinner party. But try not to sound like a used car salesman. Learn to talk in benefits. People are most interested in anything that relates back to them and their lives, so always let there be an echo of what you do for your customers. That's what people can relate to – not the "I'm the best midwife in the Southwest." That may be true, but it's not what's important.

The important element of what you really do might be that you work with nervous mothers every step of the way to ensure a natural, healthy childbirth. When you put it like that, the person you're talking to will be able to find something to relate to, and will understand the problem you solve. So, whether her sister is a nervous mother who she might not refer to you, or if she finds herself being nervous down the road, she now knows for sure who can fill this need.

Your Turn

What action steps will you take to move forward during days 40-53?

Chapter 7

Pricing, Negotiations and Collaboration –
Days 54-60

Determining your pricing structure is one of the most important decisions you'll make as a business owner. If your prices are too low, you'll work constantly and still be unable to cover your expenses; if your prices are too high, you'll be unable to acquire enough business to provide the volume that will cover your expenses. Either way, you'll be out of business before you even get started.

First off, it's important to know that you should never be afraid to charge what you're worth. If you undervalue yourself, you're giving everyone you deal with permission to undervalue you as well. It's perfectly fair to provide a service in return for a fair price. But what's a fair price?

There seems to be more leeway in determining price if you're providing a service rather than a product, but at the same time, it can be harder to justify. When you're determining the price for a product, you start with the cost and how much it takes you to make that product. But when you're providing a service, how do you put a price tag on your time and the quality of service that you're providing?

The SBA encourages you to consider three factors when calculating price.

Materials

What materials are required in order to provide your service? Are you taking blood samples that require specific disposable items? Do you need other supplies and equipment? And are these costs fixed or variable? Obviously, you only need to purchase a blood pressure monitor once, but with each customer, you'll use additional gauze, bandages and containers.

Labor

Are you providing the service or do you have employees carrying out appointments? Either way, what is the hourly rate for the service? You can factor in health insurance costs, your time, talent and convenience fees here as well. Bundle your services and charge a flat rate is the best way to get the most bang for your earned buck!

Overhead

These are your fixed monthly expenses, such as rent, Internet, utilities, advertising, insurance, mileage, etc. These should cover your current overhead expenses, so don't base this on a previous year's costs.

Taking these three factors into account, you can begin to get an idea of how to come up with your rates.

There are additional elements to consider, such as where you're positioning your brand in the market. Is your intention to be a discount service? Are you a high-end alternative or do you fall somewhere in the middle? What is the demand for your particular service? What is the going rate for what you provide? Can you offer a low, middle and high end product?

Though it's tempting to offer your services the cheapest in order to attract business, I'd avoid setting your prices based on being the least expensive option. If the only reason to choose your business is because you're the lowest price, what happens when someone new comes in and offers the same service at a cheaper price? I advise to avoid, if possible, competing solely on the platform of price. Instead, try standing out on some element of your service rather than price alone.

Someone can always come along and undercut your price, leaving you with few alternatives, but if a customer can only receive your specialized customer service, or your same day appointments from your company, they've got a reason to stay. Not to mention that pricing yourself too low undermines your perceived value. It says to your customers that you're not worth paying more for.

In contrast, charging a higher premium rate suggests and sends the message to your clients that they are paying for the best. It sets you apart as the expert in your field. Having higher prices automatically suggests to your customers that you provide a service worthy of premium pricing and so you must be the quality choice.

Also consider whether you'll be receiving payment from primary or secondary payers. How will payment work for your clients?

Will you accept health insurance and how will that determine what your payment structure should look like?

You can also determine what your pricing structure will look like based on whether you anticipate a large following or a small following. By this I mean will you be able to see a large volume of clients, or a small volume? Obviously, this also depends on the exact nature of your service, but if your business can get by on volume alone, you can afford to charge a more affordable rate. If you can only see a select group of clients, then you can charge more.

There's no harm in really sitting down and doing a little research when it comes to setting your prices.

Your pricing is going to have a great impact on your earning potential and the success of your business, and correcting your pricing once you're already into the process is not as simple as reprinting your brochure. Whenever you change prices, it should be done discreetly. There's no problem with raising your prices on a yearly or bi-yearly basis (or at least looking at them), but you don't want to be known for constantly changing your prices. If your prices are always changing, it can give the impression of instability in your business. The best practice is to make price changes as rarely as possible, but that also means that you need to be meticulous when setting them up in the first place.

Diversification

One way to meet your financial goals is to consider diversifying your offerings. I'd recommend doing some research to see if this option is a good idea for your business. It can be a good way to tap into related markets, and if done well, it could spell profits for your business. However, if done hastily, or without much consideration for the mission of your company and what your business can realistically do better than your competition, than it could scatter your interests and funds too much. I'd definitely consider it, but simply do the research to see what is in your best interest.

Identify Barriers to Sales

Sometimes, you might think you're doing everything you possibly can to generate sales, but these same things could actually prove to be barriers to sales.

DIY Websites

We spoke earlier about sites where anyone can create a website. This is a great suggestion if you have some marketing background or design background, but there is also a danger in doing your own website. Yes, it could be a lot cheaper at the outset, but it also might end up proving totally inefficient. If you can invest some time into learning a little about user experience, SEO, keywords and wire framing, it's possible to create a well-performing site, but it's important to know that web design is NOT strictly about making a good-looking or high-tech site. You want to have some sense of how users will navigate your site, how to make your offerings clear to the visitor, and how to get your visitors to take some sort of action.

The investment in time that I suggest you make, if you plan on creating an optimized website, is equal or greater to the dollar investment that you'll make when hiring someone to create your website. So, if you can't afford to invest a lot of time in getting your

DIY website right, then you should be hiring someone to do it for you. The last thing that you want is for your site to act as a deterrent to hiring you, and a site that is poorly constructed or confusing or frustrating will surely do that.

Also, a website is a like the "shingle" that you'd hang out in front of your shop. Any person passing by on the street would make a snap judgement on whether or not to walk in, based on what your shingle and front window looked like from the outside. The same is true of your online presence. If your shingle and window look cluttered, difficult to navigate or if they don't state that you can solve the visitor's problem, then that that visitor is moving on, and you've lost a sale.

Negotiating

When doing consulting work, don't be afraid to negotiate your pricing. Find out what your client needs and when. What are the parameters? Use this knowledge to determine your rate. Remember - the ideal rate is one in which both parties feel like they've won.

What does it take to be a successful negotiator? First, know that, as a nurse, you're already an expert negotiator, although you've probably never viewed it through this lens before. You negotiate when you need to get patients to take their medication. You negotiate when you need administrators to make schedule changes. You negotiate with doctors on a daily basis. So, you are not out of your element when negotiating with those who negotiate for a living, because you, too, are a master negotiator. Even so, here are some tips to keep in mind.

Start High

You can always go down, but you can't go up. You can't start low and suddenly ask for more when your first number was easily accepted. This simply won't fly. Also, know going in what you will and won't give up. Perhaps you could go down in price, but that would mean you're unable to provide any additional meetings or follow-ups.

Be Slow to Respond

Don't jump at the first offer that is given to you...even if seems reasonable. Think it over. Ask questions. Be sure of everything that is expected from you. It's not seen as unprofessional to be prudent, thorough and cautious. In fact, that in itself is a sign of an excellent negotiator.

Be Willing to Walk Away

Don't ever go into a negotiation feeling as though you need the business. Always go in from a standpoint of abundance and confidence. You don't need this job. If it's not going to be worth it and doesn't come at a fair price, then be willing to walk away. Often, it will be that very thing which will prevent the client from letting you go. But equally often, for everyone who is not willing to pay, there's someone who is willing and who will. Your job is to find those people, not to work for those who don't value you enough to give what is fair.

Don't Get Emotional

There is no room for emotions at the negotiation table. Remain calm throughout the entire process, and detach yourself from the results. If you can go in without expectations and unattached to the result, you'll find that you perform much better. It might even help to pretend that you're negotiating on behalf of someone else. Oftentimes, emotions run high because our personal wellbeing is attached to the result. But if we can view the negotiation as a business interaction, something you're doing on behalf of a competent nurse, than it will be easier to act rationally and in the best interest of that nurse (who is you).

Small Business Doesn't Mean Weak

It is easy to feel, when entering into a negotiation with an attorney or large company, that you're somehow weaker because you're just a small business, but don't let that be the case. Go in knowing the full value of what you provide and have confidence that you're worth every penny of what you're asking. Know your specific strengths when you go in and don't back down.

Small Network

Another barrier to sales might be that your network is too small. After all, is your service something that everyone needs, or is it more like something that 1 in 10 people might need? If the latter, then you'll need a considerably larger network to start seeing demand.

The easiest solution to a small network is to make it bigger. The Internet is your friend in this case, as it serves to only expand your reach regardless of how networking-averse you are. You can expand your network by joining different groups, replying to blogs, joining forums and interacting on social media. Not to mention that you can find and participate in more face-to-face networking events. Basically, always be building your network.

Constantly Be Assessing

It's important to always be on the lookout for possible barriers to your success. Ask for feedback on your website. Sometimes being so enmeshed in the building of our business, we can lose sight of simple things. For example, is your phone number easy to find on your website? Are you using the right keywords? There are many great analytics tools that will show what people are looking for on your site? Are there are other companies who serve your ideal customer (in different ways) with whom you could somehow join?

Collaborating

Collaboration with colleagues in other disciplines is a good idea, as long as it is advantageous for all involved. The purpose of collaboration is to enhance and elevate the care that you're able to provide. It is coordinated action toward a common cause and joint avocation should be the outcome.

Your Turn

What action steps will you take to move forward during days 54-60?

Chapter 8
Promotions – Days 61-70

Timeline

The key to a successful promotion is to plan ahead. Set your marketing timeline up at the start of the year and continue to look at it throughout the year. In January, you should have all of your marketing for February complete. If you are running any marketing campaigns, or if you are launching a new product or service, you should have this all planned out. You should set up a detailed plan of what ads, emails and posts are going out on which date.

Oftentimes, promotions fail because they are thrown together at the last minute. If you're offering something special for a holiday, you can't send out an email, or post an ad on social media, the day before and expect the customers to be rushing to take advantage of the promo. You have to create buzz around your product or service. Build up the hype over an extended period of time. Show up in your customers' inboxes and then continue to show up.

We receive so much advertising stimulation in our current world that not all the information gets through. We're selective about what emails we read and what links we click on. So, unless you're showing up consistently with a valuable message, chances are you'll go unnoticed.

I say this not to discourage you, but to inspire you to dig deep when you're creating promotions. Really try to get into the heads of your target audience. What email subject line would cut through the crowd and stand out? What is the real pain of your audience, and how will your promotion ease that pain?

All of this is best executed when you've taken the time to plan out your marketing campaigns and promotions and laid them out in a timeline. Having a clear timeline will also help when it comes to budget.

Marketing Budget

Attempting to run your marketing campaigns as they come up is a detriment for your marketing budget. Planning out your year allows you to see the big picture, determine your funds and decide on the smartest way to spend them. For some businesses, the bulk of sales come during the holiday season (or end of the year), so it makes sense to allocate a larger percentage of marketing dollars toward that time of year. However, if they approached marketing without looking at the entire year in advance, and simply spent money as ideas came up, they might get to Christmas and see that they've spent the entire budget.

Instead, the way to approach marketing is to look at the year in its entirety and to know ahead of time where it makes the most sense to focus the bulk of your money. Maybe summer is when you think you should put the most resources into your marketing efforts; or maybe an even spend, over the course of a year, better suits your purposes. Whatever the case, you'll know this by planning your year ahead of time.

Key dates

In your timeline, set key dates for when certain marketing must go out. If you're launching a new product or service, have a schedule of when certain posts go out, when you email, when you run a newspaper ad, when the website will be updated for that item or service, when a blog post will go up, etc. When you know the dates, you can work backwards to ensure that you have enough time to create the content.

It sounds like a lot of work to have so much planned out in advance, but in reality, all the planning will take work off your plate. Once you have everything planned, you can then automate most of what needs to happen. But it's impossible to automate when you don't have the content.

Target Audience

Just like there is a target audience for your overall business, there will also be a target audience for each promotion that you do. Not every promotion will appeal to everyone equally. And oftentimes, promotions are done to change something about a current type of customer. For example, perhaps you have a one-time client who is now on your email list, but they haven't bought anything since their first time. A promotion that will entice this person will be much different than a promotion for someone who is a regular customer.

You can take some time to figure out why some clients don't reschedule. Is it because they don't have the money, the time, or a consistent need? Try out different promotions to entice them, and see if that changes things. If they use a discount, or if they take advantage of a service that is a little different than what you normally offer, then you've answered your question. If not, you can continue to test out different promotions to see what works.

From doing promotions, you can learn a lot about your customers. Maybe once people use you, there isn't a reason to reschedule in the short term. In that case, maybe offer something in the future to those who refer you. Sometimes a client may be happy with your service, but has no further need. So, maybe asking for a referral is a great way to cash in on that good Samaritan feeling people have when they liked a service but don't have an immediate need to go back.

Email List

You'll also want to work on segmenting your email list. Blasts to everyone on your list can come across as too broad and won't appeal to everyone on the list. But as you start seeing who responds to what, and what compels your contacts to sign up to your list initially, you'll be able to start to create groups based on interests or demographics. Most email service providers will have these capabilities accessible to you on the back end. This is a smart way to increase the effectiveness of your email campaigns and promotions. Target just those customers who are the most interested in what you're offering based on their history.

Here is your Promotions Checklist

- Create a timeline for marketing promotions, creating content and product launches

- Create a marketing budget/break it down by campaign

- Determine target audience for each marketing campaign

- Begin building your email list

- Start creating and scheduling social media content

Your Turn

What action steps will you take to move forward during days 61-70?

Chapter 9
Social Media – Days 71-80

Earlier we talked about setting up your social media platforms, but what do you do once you have your accounts set up?

Growing your Network

Now that you're connected, it might be tempting to simply start posting and creating content, but unless you're connected with others in your industry, that content won't be seen. So, it makes sense that before you go crazy posting, you should first work on growing your network.

One of the easiest ways to start is by following and liking people and pages in your industry. This a great way to connect with the people and companies behind these pages and will be the posts that populate your feed. You'll be able to see what others in your industry are posting, in addition to having the opportunity to comment on these posts.

As you're just getting started, you may not have a continuous supply of your own content to share. By sharing or retweeting content from your industry peers, you're helping them extend their reach, building your own credibility and fostering good will.

If you find content that is valuable to you, it's likely that your followers will also find it valuable and the person who's content you shared will appreciate it. When you're viewed as someone who provides valuable content (whether it's yours or someone else's), you're establishing your value. Good content is always appreciated, especially if you're following, and being followed, by people in your industry and your target audience.

When you're first building your community, look to influencers in your industry who already have large communities consisting of your ideal clients. Help serve these clients by writing helpful posts and sharing information. When you share valuable information in the spirit of being helpful, they will naturally check you out. If they like what they see, they will become a part of your network. Keep up this valuable exchange of information. Thank the people who share information, and add to it when you can. The more that you interact with influencers in your industry and members of their community, the more familiar your name will become.

If this all seems tedious to you and like it's a lot of work for very little visible return, think of it like this. Most likely, you're in business because it fulfills your life's purpose. It's your path, and you feel as though you have something valuable to share or provide with people. You may think that what you have to share is the actual service that you provide people once they become a client - but you actually have much more to share than that.

You have knowledge. Expertise. Real-life anecdotes.

Your online network is a place where you can share anything in order to help people. Some will read, absorb and use what you say and may never need to call you for your services, but that's okay.

What you're building is more than just a marketing or sales funnel leading people back to you. Of course that's a goal, and that's what's going to pay your bills, but the bigger picture is that you're seeking to help people in whatever way you can. And once you position yourself as this helpful resource, you will attract more business, whether it's directly related to your efforts or just a side effect within the universe of doing what you love, and sharing what you have. You're opening yourself up to receive by the simple act of giving.

Avoid the Temptation to Over-Promote

Some people are on social media to interact, some are on to learn and others are on to simply see what everyone else is doing. But no one is on social media to be sold to. That being the case, no one is going to respond to straight up sales messages. It might seem like if you're participating in social media for your business, than you should be creating promotional marketing to send out to your followers, but this is actually not the case.

If you're going to be putting out 10 pieces of content a month, no more than 3 of those pieces should be self-promotion. That's right – the magic percentage is 30. Keep your promotional marketing to 30%. The rest of your content should be a combination of educational tips, general news about your industry and glimpses of your business behind the scenes (events, your experiences etc.). Basically, it's the presence of all of this "softer" content that is going to make it acceptable for you to send a promotional message once in a while. And, at this point, your audience is already sold on you and what you have to offer...so your message is more of a reminder rather than a cold sales pitch.

Here are some specific actions to take on various platforms:

Facebook

Find influencers in your industry on Facebook. When they post something that is relevant to your business, share their post. They will appreciate getting this extra exposure, and you will have provided quality content to those who like your page. Ideally, if you do this enough, and if you're also providing quality content, eventually those influencers will share something you post, and you will be exposed to a much larger audience. From there, others may see your content and share with their network, and on and on. This is why it is important to include in your content, a link back to your blog or website. You always want people to find their way back to your site.

Twitter

Twitter is a real-time social media platform. So, within Twitter, news happens fast. Most likely, people are following hundreds of people and brands, so anything you post is very easy to miss. That's why you need to be concise and relevant. You can follow as many related industries and businesses as you want. Not all will follow you back, but don't despair. Keep an eye on what they are posting and retweet what is relevant to your business.

Also, in the sidebar, Twitter will show you what hashtags are currently trending. If you can work any of these into a message that is relevant for your business, this might give your post a larger audience. Also, check the Twitter pages of your influencers. What hashtags do they use? Can you jump into the conversation on any of these hashtags? Try to participate in 2-3 tweet chats per week.

Instagram

Instagram is all about images and less about the words. How can your business use images to add value to your brand? Take a look at what others in your industry are doing on Instagram. What hashtags are they using? How many followers do they have? Follow people in your industry and chime in on relevant posts.

Also try to find a unique angle for your business. Instagram skews in the direction of a younger demographic than Facebook and Twitter, so you can afford to show off the youthful side of your business. Your demeanor should be consistent with your overall brand, but you can loosen up a bit on Instagram. If you travel to your clients and are focused on pediatrics, maybe you have a little mascot that you bring along with you. So maybe you dedicate your Instagram to the places that little mascot has been and share photos of the mascot in various locations throughout the week.

Your photos don't have to be just from what you're actually doing, but could be images related to your specialty. If your niche is skin care, maybe you show images related to different foods or drinks that are good for the skin. The possibilities are unlimited. Don't be afraid to show off your artistic side.

LinkedIn

On LinkedIn, you'll create a company page in addition to your personal profile. Then you'll update your status so that your position is owner or founder of your particular company. If you plan on posting short, informative articles, you can do so through your company page. From you personal LinkedIn page, you can then send invites to people in your region with roles similar to yours. When they accept your connection (based on the similarity in your industry), they may click to learn more about the company, so make sure your company page is complete.

Also, once they accept your invitation, send them a short, sweet note thanking them for accepting. LinkedIn is the platform most like a business networking meeting, so you'll see that users are happy to make new connections with those in their industry.

Schedule Time for Social Media Marketing

The network that you're growing and the connections that you're making through social media can be time-consuming. Much of what you'll be doing is small, quick tasks, but by the time you do them all, you can feel like you've just squandered the day away on social media. For this reason, it's important for you to come up with a plan and a schedule. Set aside specific blocks of time to attend to your social media tasks. It can be so easy to get distracted in one direction or another as you're creating and reacting to posts, so come up with specific daily, weekly and monthly goals and stick to them.

These goals could be anything as long as they give you a sense of purpose and something specific to accomplish. You can set a goal of how many people to interact with in a specific time period, or determine how many posts you want to create. Maybe you decide you want to update your cover photos every two months, or denote a particular amount of time that you want to spend simply researching what others are saying and doing. Whatever you decide, make it a task or group of tasks that is measurable so that you know when you're done. Don't just poke around on your social media sites with no particular aim. That's not likely to grow your network or make you feel good about the time you've spent online.

Content Development

This leads me into content development. Where do you start and how do you find the time to create content?

Many small business owners find this especially tough because creating quality content is so time-consuming, and they are not in the business of content creation. It might seem like a great idea in theory, but your day is most likely spent largely with clients or doing the actual business. When will you have time to, essentially, take on another job - the job of online marketing and content creation?

Well, it's true. It is a lot of work, especially in the beginning. But here are some tips you can use that will make your content development much easier.

Blogging

Blogging is a great way to get in front of your potential customers on a regular basis, but, at the same time, it's a whole lot of writing. There are a few different approaches you can take when it comes to blogging. If you created your own website, or had someone create it for you through WordPress or Squarespace, your service might allow you to have a blog page on your website. If this is the case, and you or your developer can add that page and give you access, you can start blogging right from there.

You could also start a blog on a completely separate URL through a blogging site, but I would steer you away from that direction. The reason for this is that your blog, especially if it's rich in SEO content and updated frequently, is going to draw traffic. If it's not directly connected to your website, you're losing precious views to your website. Also, when people go to your website and see a blog link, it's often one of the first places they will go. Here, they can get an immediate sense of who you are when you're not speaking in your polished web content voice. Basically, if your website is your business card or shop sign, then your blog is like the conversation someone has with you after you hand them your card, or once they walk into your shop. In that respect, your blog is going to be a more persuasive tool than your website.

Once you have 5-6 articles of about 500-1000 words, you can start blogging. Get into a routine, and post once a week. Mondays are great days to post your blog. Something about late morning on a Monday makes people want to read blogs. A Google search about when it's best to blog will produce plenty of information. And once you get going, you can experiment a little yourself to see if your particular audience feels the same way.

If the thought of writing a blog post completely turns your stomach, you can always hire someone to write for you. Jot down ideas for topics throughout the day, or as they come to you, and then you can go onto sites like Fiverr.com or guru.com to find writers for an affordable price. With a list of ideas or an outline, they can churn out content when you can't...or don't want to. Once you find a writer whose style aligns with yours, they will be more than happy to have a consistent writing gig with you.

Many probably have some experience with SEO writing and social media marketing, so as your brand grows, you can hire them to do all of that for you. So that's something to look forward to once your business gets off the ground.

Videos

Video tutorials are an extremely powerful method of content marketing, and they are also easier to create than you might think. All you really need is a smartphone, or a laptop, to get started. Once you create your videos, you can upload them to your Youtube page and post them to all of your social media accounts, as well. Sometimes, they even work as part of your blog. You can write a few paragraphs and supplement with a video.

If you're making a simple tutorial, Youtube provides some editing tools that allow you to edit text and add music or links. If you want to get fancier, iMovie, on a Mac, or Windows Moviemaker, on a PC, are easy and free to use.

Other Content

There are many other types of content, in addition to blogs and videos, in which you can dabble or jump into, depending on how relevant they are to your business and whether or not you enjoy creating them. There are free online resources where you can create quizzes or surveys to send out via social media or email. You can create infographics or PDFs full of information. You could even start a podcast, or create a course. You don't have to do all of these things at once, but know that you are not restricted to blogging. There are many options, and once you get going you'll start to see what your followers enjoy. Do more of that. When you notice that a piece of content you created is getting shared or being interacted with, try to create more things like that.

Also, remember that a great deal of your content can be recycled. Don't simply create content, use it once and then surrender it to an archived folder on your desktop. Use that content again, or reformat it for a different medium. Turn a blog post into a video, or a tip sheet into an infographic. If you blog about one topic frequently, maybe you have enough info to turn it into an ebook, or PDF guide that you can give away free on your website to attract new email subscribers.

Think of your content arsenal as your fridge. You don't just make a meal once and then throw away the leftover ingredients. No, you get creative. Maybe you take the extra produce from last night's dinner and make an omelet so things don't go to waste. You're doing the same thing with your content. Always brainstorm ways that you can re-purpose what you have. Feel free to simply re-post something that you posted a while ago. If you had a blog post that was a hit, or even if it wasn't because your network was still small, it doesn't hurt to repost down the road when your network is bigger. Chances are it wasn't seen or was forgotten, so make a few edits, change the picture and you're good to go. Simply state, flat out, that you're repeating old content under the guise of a "throwback" or a "back by popular request."

When you run out of ideas for content, try to think about why your customers follow and interact with you. What are they looking for? What do they look forward to? You can even ask them in a simple email, or get fancier with a formal survey. The answers might surprise you. Connect again with why you're here and what you're doing all of this for. People like online presences who are real people with real passion. If you are producing content and information that is in line with your mission and who you are as a person, your audience will connect. Interact with them as if they were in your living room or your church. Remember this when you're lost for what to post next. Reconnect with your purpose.

Workflows and Standard Operating Procedures

As I've hinted at in the previous section, you'll need to establish different workflows and operating procedures in order to be successful. Just as in life, what you don't pay attention to won't grow, or at least it won't grow well. For your business, as a whole, to be successful, you must pay attention to each aspect. If you ignore your taxes and accounting, it will be a mess when you look at it once a year. If you ignore your social media for large chunks of time, you won't be able to grow and maintain an active audience, and your efforts will fall flat.

Therefore, it's important to lay out all of the things that require your attention, determine how often they need your attention and create a schedule that allows you to spend time working on these elements. Whenever you can streamline something, or automate something, do it. Come up with a set procedure for your process of acquiring a new lead and booking and invoicing a client. If a part of your process doesn't work, change it. You don't have to know the best processes from the start, but you do need to know when it could be improved or should be abandoned. Don't be afraid to experiment and change until you get it right.

And stick to your schedule. You are your own boss, so that means you have to get yourself to sit down and take care of the administrative parts of the business -because you need to. Obviously, as the boss, you can also tell yourself that you can take a half day or save something for tomorrow, but that boss won't be in business very long if this is common practice. Be smart about creating a schedule that works for both you and the business.

Your schedule and the operating procedures that you set up will keep you on track and moving toward your goals. Most times, when given the choice, we as humans will choose to do the task that we like the best. But a smart entrepreneur does the thing that will have the biggest effect – the task that's worth the most. You can even arrange your to-do list in this manner. What are the tasks with the biggest payoffs? What are maintenance items? What will garner new business? When you organize your priorities in this way, it becomes clearer how to structure your time so that you're doing less busywork and achieving more results.

Your Turn

What action steps will you take to move forward during days 71-80?

Chapter 10
Product Creation – Days 81-89

If you're a savvy entrepreneur, you're probably already thinking about how you can expand your business beyond just the services you offer. After all, any service you provide is directly linked to your time and energy, which is a fixed denomination. You can't work or take more clients than you can physically see. So, even if you had a client in every available slot, you'd see your salary cap. This couldn't really change unless you raised your prices. So, how could you augment your revenue without working yourself to the ground or forever escalate your prices?

The answer is - selling products! Products are an excellent way to increase your revenue because they are unrelated to your time and energy. Therefore, the earning potential in a product, versus your service, is unlimited. And it's a passive income, meaning you could be earning money while you sleep, or on vacation.

But what kind of products can you provide as an entrepreneurial nurse? There are two choices – Information Products and Physical Products.

Information Products

Information products are the easiest to create, produce and sell. And because so much is done online, you don't even need to send a physical product to a customer. Your website will take care of everything.

But what do I mean by "information product?"

An information product is, essentially, information packaged in an easy-to-consume format. There are lots of different options, such as ebooks, checklists, tip booklets, audio or video e-courses, video tutorials and more.

Basically, you'll come up with a theme or topic that is closely tied to your business expertise. You've already been working on social media and within your content marketing to establish yourself as an expert in your particular niche. This is a way to further drive this point home. The content that you've been sharing for free on social media is what reinforces your expertise in your audience's eyes, so when they see that you sell even more in-depth information on your website, they will already trust you and be that much closer to a sale.

This is the goal of giving away high quality free material and email series, where people can learn about whatever it is that you are an expert. If you set up your website to have a pop-up offering a free Tip Booklet if they provide their email, they are already a well-qualified lead for any additional information products that you might provide. You can then send these contacts exclusive offers to join your e-course before you release it to the public. Or, you can send them a holiday promo code so that they can get a special discount to a particular resource that might interest them.

Whatever information products you set up and promote, they are passive income. Once you create these items once, you don't have to touch them again. You can simply sell them. And if you do eventually want to update them, you totally can at minimal or no cost, because they are not physical products.

Basically, you are helping people in your ideal field without expending time and energy. And if you work this end of your business hard enough, by extending your reach and growing your network, you might be able to discontinue your service business altogether if you'd like. Wouldn't that be an amazing transition from your current or former burnout?

The only limit to the products you can sell is your own imagination. Great ways to generate ideas for information products is to jot down, or consider the questions you had to Google. What resource do you wish was out there for people in your position? Check to see what common keyword searches are in your industry. If they don't exist, or if it does exist and you can do it better, create it. You're most likely not the only one with a particular question. So, if you can put together all the information that you struggled to find and turn it into an information product, you are filling a need. Once you set up your online presence and start driving traffic to your site, you'll be helping a large population and will be making a passive income from it.

Physical Products

The other option for selling products is to sell actual products. Opting for this option will largely depend on what your specific nursing niche is, because it might be a natural extension of what you're doing. Perhaps it makes sense to offer your service and to also have a corresponding line of products to somehow complement that service.

The downside to physical products is that it will cost money to create them and to ship them. But if your margins are large enough, and if there is a demand for these products, then it could be a worthwhile investment.

When it comes to selling either information products or physical products, there are plenty of websites and resources out there to help you sell your products online. Shopify is a popular ecommerce website. There are also website hosting platforms that give you the ability to create and provide e-courses and craft landing pages for each product. There's definitely a lot of potential for selling your products online.

Live Events

Live events are related to products in the value that they provide, but will extend your reach and serve as a platform to sell even more products. But more importantly, they serve to help your customers engage with you on a more personal and real level. They strengthen the link between you and your customers, and help position you as more reputable and knowledgeable in your field.

You might be wondering, how is my nursing business related to live events? At first it might seem like two entirely unrelated career paths, but depending on the logistics of your business, it could be the fuel for your nursing business and vice versa.

The expertise that is uniquely yours is your entryway into the world of live events. The content that you're providing on a regular basis through your social media platforms, the e-books, courses, checklists and workbooks that you've created are all precursors to live events. You are creating and nurturing a following every time that you post and blog and interact with your community. And if you have anything to say that others need to know, you have value to provide - value for which people will pay.

The place to start is online. You can host webinars where you either get in front of your webcam and talk to your audience or you can style the webinar where participants can only see your screen and you go through your points in a PowerPoint style. Either way, you're, in effect, providing a teaser of what a live event would be like with you in person. But at the same time, you are providing your following with content that you can only get by working with you.

So, when you are designing your webinars and marketing in general, you should always be thinking about where your expertise lies. What can you offer people that no one else can? What have you discovered throughout your career that could make someone else's journey easier? What problems did you run into on your journey that you could help others avoid?

Find out what those problem points are, and provide the solution. What, when you were dealing with it, if someone had said, "attend my webinar for the solution." Would you have leapt at the chance to attend? That's what you need to be teaching to others. Make sure that you are recording your webinars. Don't charge for your webinar and then assume that you have to create another one in order to generate a profit again. You can continue to profit from the recordings of webinars for years to come. You can offer access to recordings after they've happened, or compile them into an e-course that you mail out when people sign up for your newsletter. Once they are recorded and exist, they are content that you can reformat to reuse. Definitely continue to leverage those recordings in the future for as long as the information is relevant. You could even use the webinars as the gateway to your live event.

People attend webinars for information that they didn't have before. They want insight and they believe they can find it by attending your live webinar, or watching older webinar recordings, but they come to live events for a deeper reason. As you move into hosting live events, you can't simply provide the information that you provided online. People get up and out of their houses, book flights and reserve hotel rooms in order to be inspired. They want to hear the untold stores, the stories that they'll never hear unless they're sitting in a room with you. They want to know exactly how you got where you are because, likely, they are trying to get themselves to a similar place but are facing hurdles and adversity. Or they just don't know where to start.

As you start to market your live event, you'll want to pique potential customers' interest by giving them a taste of the inspiration they'll find when they attend your event. A great way to do this is to have mini virtual events where you get people excited about what they can expect. You can create a tiered pricing strategy that you present at the end of the mini events where you have early bird admission available but that will go up soon. Each time you post a mini virtual event on social media or your landing page, keep the price low for a certain window and then raise it in order to incentivize people to take advantage of the low rate.

Another good idea is to launch your live event with a 2-for-1 deal. This means that early adopters will be motivated to bring a friend. In a live event scenario, having guests there with friends will increase the positivity and good feelings in the room (and fill up more seats)! Also, when you have sets of friends in your crowd, it will increase the chance of picture taking and sharing on social media. People are more likely to start conversations, participate and reach out to new contacts when they are with one person who they already know.

Remember that your live event starts when customers purchase their ticket online, months in advance. At this point you should make sure that you have an automated campaign set up to keep them in the loop about event preparations, itineraries, location details and any other helpful information. Maybe even send some complimentary content to amp them up even more.

Of course, don't inundate their inbox with too many emails, but definitely stay in touch. If they signed up and are attending, they are definitely interested in what you have to say, so they'll be excited to get relevant emails about the upcoming event.

Your guests want to leave inspired and ready to implement the action points that you've shared with them during the event. And their testimonials will also be vital to your future events, so be sure to collect feedback. You can hire a videographer to get real live clips while the event is happening, or you can send out a survey after the fact. You could even do a combination of both.

If you have physical products to sell, like books, t-shirts or CDs, your event is a great place to make these available. As long as the purpose of your event is not pure sales (guests will definitely see through this), your products will be welcome, especially if they are extensions of what you discussed, or are tools to help them take the next step.

Your Turn

What action steps will you take to move forward during days 81-89?

Chapter 11
Get a Mentor – Day 90

Find a Mentor or Coach

The hardest part of starting any business is the fact that, often, you're doing it alone. You can find the answer to almost any question online, but it's difficult to differentiate between what's good and what's sub-par. It's also pretty common to find conflicting information. How can you tell what's right for you and your circumstances? How can you avoid the cookie-cutter answer that might not exactly fit your situation? There is definitely something to be said for having a real person to talk to when questions arise or problems surface.

If you research the most successful people in the world, you'll see that they all had mentors. Maya Angelou mentored Oprah. Steve Jobs mentored Mark Zuckerburg. Ray Charles mentored Quincy Jones. Basically, if they are famous enough that you know their name, they probably had a mentor.

Mentors are not just people who can coach you in times of distress. They have experience, and experience is an expensive commodity. In fact, experience is the one thing that you can't buy.

You can read, you can study, you can research, but there is no alternative to experience. The only way to get experience is to live through it. A mentor can provide you with business advice from the perspective of experience. In fact, having a mentor is the only real way to benefit from experience before living through it.

In addition to the general business acumen and problem-solving that comes from experience, your mentor also has a network. Your mentor knows more people than you because he or she has been in the game longer. It's like moving to a new town. It would take you months or years to get to know, through experience, where to take your car to get it fixed, or which salon is the best. And you would have no cause to know certain things until you actually needed them. You would have no use in knowing which realtor to use until you were ready to purchase a home.

Similarly, a mentor has been places that you have had no need to be yet so they already know who to call for what problem. They've already dealt with situations that are, as of now, only in your future. Therefore, not only will they be able to recommend you to these resources, they will also be able to make connections that you didn't even know were possible. By having a mentor, you are leveraging an entirely different network and becoming part of it. Having a mentor is like getting a head start in business.

Also, on the surface, it might seem like the primary reason to have a mentor is to have someone to help with your questions and the problems that come up as you make your way as an entrepreneur. But that's actually the secondary reason. That reason stems from the fact that we are scared as we make our way down this path of entrepreneurship. We're scared of what we'll encounter, or that we won't do things correctly or that we'll mess up somehow.

What we forget is that it is only the nuts and bolts. These things are all important and helpful, but what a mentor provides that we cannot even imagine at the outset is the grain of inspiration, the extra push of encouragement and that added bit of confidence. Having a mentor is not primarily about having someone on our side to help us see what's wrong, but with having someone in our corner who can propel us to think a little bit bigger, take a calculated risk or push ourselves outside of our comfort zone to achieve greatness.

A mentor not only knows what it takes to succeed monetarily, but also what it takes to succeed emotionally, mentally and spiritually. Decisions will undoubtedly arise down the line to which there is no right or wrong answer. It could be in regard to how best to deal with a client, or what particular path to take at a challenging business crossroad. Having a mentor in those circumstances can illuminate the course of action that is right for you as a person. The ethical dilemmas, the situations that seem to pry at your moral fiber and the job-related problems that can have big repercussions on your personal life are the instances where mentors provide the brightest light. In these instances, a mentor can be an absolute blessing.

So, having a mentor is not what people do when they can't do it themselves, or don't have the right resources. People have mentors because it opens up a new world for them, amplifies the possibilities and increases the chance for grander thought and wilder success. Having a mentor can only increase your chance for success, and undoubtedly, will make whatever success you would've found on your own that much more expansive.

I know the nursing industry inside and out, and have mentored nurse entrepreneurs like you, who now are thriving and living abundant lives. It fills my heart for me to see them doing what they love and being successful. I'm ready to be your mentor and to help you on your path to RNterprising. It's a wonderful experience to do what you love and to do it on your own schedule. And it's even more wonderful to watch the people who I coach go through this same transition.

It starts with just the seed of an idea and an urge to do what you love, without the unneeded stress. I've helped nurture this urge in its infancy and watched my mentees set up original, creative and successful businesses where they no longer answer to the demands of the hospital hierarchy. You can create an RNterprise that's satisfying for you AND beneficial to your clients.

Once connecting with me and completing your 90 day start up, you will also have access to my Secret Mastermind Circle (SMC). This is where mentees are placed with other business owners who might be performing in the particular type of business that you desire to run. I have connected with just a few entrepreneurs in Healthcare. The group and its representatives grow daily.

We have entrepreneurs representing the following to help you in the Mastermind:

Home Health Care Agency

Adult Day Care Center

Group Home

Nurse Travel Agency

Staffing Agency

CPR Instructors

Medicare/Medicaid Experts

Banking Representative

Non-Profit Expert

Business Plan Writer

Legal Nurse Consultant

CNA School Owner

Together, let's make your dream a reality. Let's get moving toward your success. Connect with me and, in 90 days, your dream can be well on its way to becoming reality.

Once the business is started, I will continue to mentor and teach you how to build upon each one that will comprise your RNterprise.

This RNterprise leads to your Legacy.

Your legacy is something your family will forever be grateful that you started for years to come.

Get started today and schedule time to meet with me at:

Michellerhodesonline.com

Your Turn

What action steps will you take to move forward on day 90?

Chapter 12
Conclusion

As you can see, we've covered a lot of material. Starting and maintaining your own business is not an easy task. If it were, everyone would be doing it. It is, however, an extremely rewarding path, one that is empowering and liberating. RNterprising is the way to transform your experience and love for nursing into your true life's purpose.

It's one thing to provide care and compassion as a nurse in a hospital setting, but the piece that is missing is YOU, your wellbeing, your health, your true calling. RNterprising is the marriage of the two. There is a place where both you and your clients can be healthy and fulfilled. And YOU can create it.

This book is just the tip of the iceberg as far as what I can offer you in getting your own RNterprise off the ground. I want to help you realize your dreams, dissolve your burnout and replace it with something a hundred times more fulfilling and just as, if not more, lucrative.

If this book has inspired you to take action, or if you'd like even more support in your journey, I am here to help. This Rhodes leads to your success!

"Remember, with God all things are possible"

To learn more about me, Michelle Rhodes, and my coaching program, please visit my website: michellerhodesonline.com

Speak with you soon! Coach Michelle

About the Author

Michelle Greene Rhodes is known as THE Life Coach and Business Consultant for Nurse Entrepreneurs.

Inspired by her passion, she assists Health Professionals who struggle with the "start-up" phase of their business. She helps them free up their time, and find a purpose filled life of their own by streamlining the first steps of entrepreneurship.

Michelle graduated Nursing school at age 21 from Florida A&M University and completed graduate school at age 27 from University of Central Florida with her Masters in Health Administration. She has gone on to enjoy a 20 year career in Nursing and has decided to enter into entrepreneurship and take a few others along the way!

Described as an intellectual and compassionate caregiver, Michelle conveys caring, empowerment and optimism in everything that she does. Many nurses over the years have stated they learned so much from Michelle and enjoyed being around her encouraging personality.

Having become a Certified Mentor and Life Coach, she decided to immerse herself in servant leadership, giving back to those who needed the most, while starting up a business. "So many times, I had 1000 questions and very few answers," states Michelle. "I knew this was a problem that needed to be filled because, as nurses, we are taught how to care within our specialty, but only if you're very lucky will you encounter a Veteran nurse to help you find the answers that you need on your personal journey to entrepreneurship."

Michelle is active on all social media platforms, with avid followers.

She is an author and speaker and looks forward to releasing her first book on May 20, 2017 in Tampa, Florida, at her First Annual Health and Wealth Brunch for Health Care Professionals.

Michelle is very active in her community as an engaged and industrious member of the nonprofit The National Coalition of 100 Black Women as the Co-Chair of Health (Tampa, Florida Chapter), and also sits on the Mayors African American Advocacy Council (MAAAC) in Tampa Florida.

She also is the Founder of the Tampa Chapter of Black Nurses Rock, Inc., a non-profit organization. She serves as a Certified Mentor and Wellness Coach.

She is the loving, devoted wife of retired Air Force Veteran, Albert Rhodes Jr. and a proud, loving mother of Jon and Ali.